Oz & James
DRINK TO BRITAIN

Oz & James
DRINK TO BRITAIN

Oz Clarke and James May

With Martin and Simon Toseland

PAVILION

First published in the United Kingdom in 2009
by Pavilion Books

An imprint of Anova Books Company Ltd
10 Southcombe Street
London W14 0RA

Produced in association with RDF Television, part of the RDF
Media Group Ltd,
The Gloucester Building, Kensington Village, Avonmore Road,
London W14 8RF

Commissioning Editor: Fiona Holman
Art Director: Lee-May Lim
Layout, design and typesetting: Thameside Media
Copy Editor: Maggie Ramsay
ISBN 978-1-86205-846-0

A CIP catalogue record for this book is
available from the British Library

10 9 8 7 6 5 4 3 2 1

Reproduction by Dot Gradations, London
Printed and bound by Mondadori, Italy

www.anovabooks.com

CONTENTS

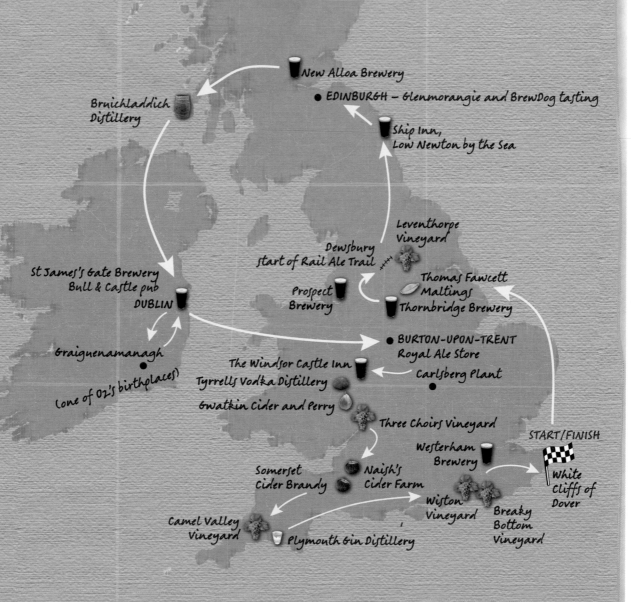

A MAP SHOWING OUR
ROUTE AROUND
BRITAIN AND IRELAND

New Alloa Brewery

EDINBURGH – Glenmorangie and BrewDog tasting

Bruichladdich
Distillery

Ship Inn,
Low Newton by the Sea

Leventhorpe
Vineyard

Dewsbury
start of Rail Ale Trail

Thomas Fawcett
Maltings
Thornbridge Brewery

St James's Gate Brewery
Bull & Castle pub
DUBLIN

Prospect
Brewery

BURTON-UPON-TRENT
Royal Ale Store

Graiguenamanagh

Carlsberg Plant

(one of OZ's birthplaces)

The Windsor Castle Inn
Tyrrells Vodka Distillery
Gwatkin Cider and Perry

Three Choirs Vineyard

START/FINISH

Westerham
Brewery

White
Cliffs of
Dover

Somerset
Cider Brandy

Naish's
Cider Farm

Wiston
Vineyard

Breaky
Bottom
Vineyard

Camel Valley
Vineyard

Plymouth Gin Distillery

BRITAIN THROUGH A GLASS

Welcome to Oz & James Drink to Britain

– an account of our thinly disguised drinking holiday through Britain and Ireland, and what we found out about British booze en route.

The idea was really very simple. We've been to France, we've been to California, we've enjoyed the wines, James has learnt a lot about viticulture, and Oz has learnt that James can't spit. It seemed only right to take a look closer to home, and go in search of the drink that defines modern Britain.

James: This was largely Oz's idea and conceived in a pub, and because we'd been in a pub, I agreed to it. It was a triumph of beer over experience.

There's no doubting that we Brits stand at a particularly interesting point in our relationship with the booze. Pubs are closing at a dizzying rate, rubbish lager dominates drink sales, yet there are definite signs of a revival in indigenous drinking culture, the likes of which have not been seen before.

Oz: These days you can't move for experts warning you about drinking, and it's all so extreme. On the one hand it's about the health effects, the social effects, the fact that civilisation is collapsing because of 'binge-drinking' — a few rampant teenagers knocking back their own weight in lager on a Saturday night.

James: And on the other hand there's café society: the increasing sophistication of our middle classes, huddling under an umbrella on a town centre pavement, discussing the attributes of a cheeky little Sauvignon from Chile, while knocking back alcohol like a performing seal swallows fish. Of course, most drinks news reporting is pants, and drink has always been good for a scandal.

So part of our mission was to defend the right of normal British people to get a bit pissed. Look at us — it hasn't done us any harm.

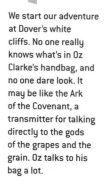

We start our adventure at Dover's white cliffs. No one really knows what's in Oz Clarke's handbag, and no one dare look. It may be like the Ark of the Covenant, a transmitter for talking directly to the gods of the grapes and the grain. Oz talks to his bag a lot.

Normal Brits enjoying perfectly normal activities after some rather good English ales — no harm done, see?

8

Oz: Mild drunkenness is one of the charming things about the British nation. Everyone has a few beers, gets slightly lit up and we're all smiling. Slightly drunk, fine; what's wrong with that?

James: British drinking culture has had a profound effect on making us the nation we are. It might well be said that beer and tea helped put the 'Great' into 'GB'.

Oz: That's true. And we'll be looking at a bit of the history – fascinating stuff. For starters, we've got beer to thank for civilisation in this great country of ours – when our ancestors realised that you could get stocious by fermenting berries each autumn with the wild yeasts that buzz in the air around us, and then realised you could do the same with grain all year round, they decided to put down roots and get brewing. It was beer, not bread, that led to the first permanent settlements in Britain.

James: Of course, the Romans tried to turn our heads with their fancy wines. They planted a lot of vineyards when they arrived here over two thousand years ago, but us unruly Brits said, 'No thanks, we'll stick with the ale. And a bag of nuts.'

Beer and tea made us a nation of inventors and engineers; in Britain we have an inherent ability to build things – oh yes we do.

James: And the Industrial Revolution — that wouldn't have happened if we weren't a nation of beer and tea drinkers. You can't invent things on coffee and wine. Coffee makes you too jittery and wine mellows you too much. James Watt didn't think, 'Oh, I'll invent the steam engine this afternoon, after I've polished off a carafe of Chardonnay for lunch.'

Oz: And, if it wasn't for the Industrial Revolution, we very likely wouldn't have climate change, which brings us back full circle, because without global warming we wouldn't be able to celebrate the increasing viability of Britain for seriously good viticulture.

Yes, since the 1950s, Britain has experienced a renaissance in vine-growing. It's been a painful road (though very good for dentists and antacid manufacturers), but the results are finally beginning to taste impressive. We had to get out and about and see how our

The Spirit of Ecstasy's upturned wings were originally intended as a sort of sighting device for clattered toffs and inbreds.

top producers are faring, and how their wines compared with those made by our more established friends in France and California. Are these people dreamers, with more money than sense and an eccentric obsession that will never bear fruit, or are they trailblazers for a whole new drinking culture in which British regions will achieve the status of Burgundy, Napa Valley and Champagne on the global wine map?

We also wanted to find out how such a change might affect our relationship with the pint, that bastion of British drinking culture. There's a new generation of beer brewers, who are recreating some of the finest beer styles in British history.

James rinses off the Royce with some unwanted French sparkling wine.

James: But it doesn't stop there. Other drinks that might define modern Britain include whisky, of course, gin, vodka – and did we mention cider? So we set off, in that supremely British combination of the Rolls Royce and the caravan, to find out the truth about booze in Britain.

Oz: And tea.

James: Well, yes, and tea.

what's all this BEER then?

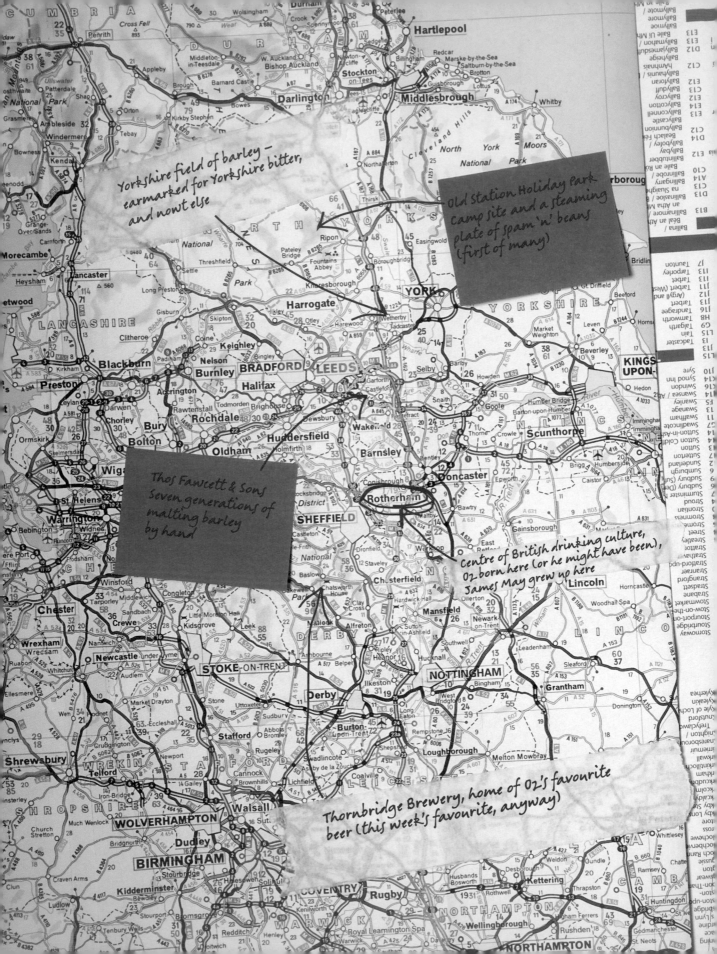

Yorkshire field of barley – earmarked for Yorkshire bitter, and nowt else

Old station Holiday Park camp site and a steaming plate of spam 'n' beans (first of many)

Thos Fawcett & Sons seven generations of malting barley by hand

Centre of British drinking culture, Oz born here (or he might have been), James May grew up here

Thornbridge Brewery, home of Oz's favourite beer (this week's favourite, anyway)

CHAPTER 1: WHAT'S ALL THIS BEER THEN?

As we are in search of the drinks that speak for modern Britain, beer really has to be the first round on our agenda. Just as wine is *absolument* French, so beer is quintessentially British.

Beer is entering another critical period in its august history, with pubs closing down at the rate of 36 a week, but there are signs of a resurgence of fine craft beers, so-called **'real ales'**. Microbreweries are flourishing and traditional ale-making skills are being kept alive by a dedicated band of beer fanatics. It was our intention to make their acquaintance and learn a little more about what they do. We know pubs are closing – but good pubs? Good locals, community pubs – are they closing or thriving? We were delighted to take on the challenge of finding out the truth.

But first we needed to learn what was in a beer, and why. Beer, or ale as it was originally called, has been around for thousands of years, and although our ancestors weren't equipped with state-of-the-art brewing equipment, they still managed to get clattered on a Saturday night. How? Well it's all to do with the basic ingredients of beer: malted barley, yeast, water and, in more recent times, hops. We set off to discover our beer roots.

Our first stop, appropriately enough, is a field of barley. Barley is the basis of most beers, but can lay claim to much, much more. Yes, barley, that humble cereal grain, may be considered the reason for civilisation as we know it.

Why? Well, a short science lesson is in order.

OZ CLARKE'S BARLEY LESSON

for fat heads

Barley is an old wild grass with grains full of starch. Each spring, to create a new root and a new barley plant, the starch has to turn into sugar to feed the root that it sets down. At that time, wild yeasts in the air are going to attack the sugar and turn it into alcohol if they can. That's why there's a husk on the plant – to prevent the yeasts getting to the sugar.

But if you gather all the barley grains together, to make bread for instance, and shove them into pots kept out in the open, and it rains and then the sun comes out and it warms up again, each little husk of barley is going to believe it's springtime and think 'Hey! Got to transform that starch into sugar so I can grow my roots.'

Now, hunter-gatherers in olden days would look at that barley and think, 'Oh, this has gone a bit sweet and mushy, but I'll try a few handfuls.' The next morning they would wake up and wonder, 'Why was I dancing on the table? Why does my head hurt?' Anyway, once they realised what was happening, the old ways lost some of their

James's tasting note: Barley tastes like one of those really left-wing health bars you get from petrol stations – deliberately kept in a state of misery. It looks a bit like a prawn.

appeal. Their wives would say, 'Aren't you off hunter-gathering today?' and they would reply, 'No darling, I'm going to stick around here and plant some barley.'

So they would harvest the barley, and store the grains in pots. They discovered that if you wet the husks, then dry them, the starch transforms into sugar. If you then crush them and mix them with water, the wild yeasts in the air convert the sugar into alcohol – and, as if by some miracle, you've suddenly got ale.

People started living in places, in communities, not because they wanted to build houses but because they wanted to grow barley to brew beer, and once in communities they started writing poetry, and symphonies, and invented the steam engine, and started going on caravan holidays – and that is civilisation.

James's

GRAIN FACT!

"A desire to drink beer and get wellied was what brought us together as people to live in communities. Also, because drinking allows ugly and boring people to have sex with each other, that means that the population flourished as well – because of beer!"

wheel (ish)

And what's more, barley can be stored throughout the year

shed

Because the grain stores itself in the husk – its own little shed

Exactly! It's a brilliant natural creator of happiness! It won't go rotten like apples or grapes. With wine, you can only make it once a year!

beer

So we can truthfully claim that civilisation was created by a desire to brew beer.

JAMES:

To précis all that, primitive man took the barley grain, worked out how to get drunk, and the next thing we have is an Andy Capp cartoon, and that's why there aren't enough shelves in the world. Far from beer being the ruin of society, as some people would claim, it's actually the bedrock of it.

Next up we visit **Thomas Fawcett Maltings in Castleford**, West Yorkshire, to find out from the malt master, James Fawcett, how the grains of barley are turned into a 'malt', ready to be made into beer.

Pale Ale Malt

Caramalt

Crystal Malt

Amber Malt

Chocolate Malt

Black Malt

Barley grain provides the fermentable sugars in most beers, but it has to be 'malted' by soaking it in water, allowing it to begin germination, and then drying the partially germinated grain in a kiln. Malting the barley produces enzymes that convert starches in the grain into fermentable sugars. Different roasting times and temperatures produce different colours of malt from the barley. **Darker malts will produce darker beers.** Got that? Thought not. Let's try again.

There are different ways to make the malt, but here they show us a traditional method, which they have been using for 200 years. James Fawcett explains what the objective of malting the grain is:

Messrs Fawcett and May deep in a malty conversation. Fawcett is the tidy looking chap.

MR FAWCETT:

What we're trying to do in the malting process is convert the insoluble starch in the barley corn into a soluble form of starch and enzymes – the fermentable sugars. The way you do that is by starting to 'grow' the grain, so the cell walls break down during the growing process and all the energy is released.

MR MAY:

So you've tricked it into believing it's spring? So you've misled millions and millions of husks of barley?

Malt can be roasted and that affects the colour and flavour of the finished beer. There are pale malts, amber and red crystal malts, chocolate and black malts. Together, they can be used to produce an irrelevant but artistic picture of several beers in a variety of hues, many of them out of focus.

THE MALTING PROCESS

"

We germinate the grains for seven days on the floor, which is the ancient way. When we have reached the optimum conversion of the starches in the grain, we take the grain to a kiln and it is kilned at high temperatures for three days, which reduces the moisture content; we end up with a very dry, friable – or crunchy – product and the inside of the malt grain will then be very sweet. Once we've done that it is ready to be sent off to a brewer.

The first thing he does is grind it up in a mill and then put hot water on it again. In the brewing process the sweet malt liquid is called 'wort' – what you get when you add water to your milled malt – it's the colour of beer but it's a very sweet, sugary liquid. You then add hops to the wort, boil it up and put it into a fermenting vessel. Then it is cooled down, yeast is added, which feeds off the sugars in the malt, and that's what gives you your beer, your alcohol, your flavour and colour – with the hops adding their unique extra bitterness and aroma.

"

James Fawcett is optimistic about the future of the British pint:

'I think the UK beer drinker is becoming a more sophisticated person – there is a huge amount of choice from craft brewers and far more interest in specialist, local beers.'

FAWCETT'S
MALT
"PUTTING QUALITY INTO A PINT"

James: Floor malt is very comfortable. It's like a down mattress that moulds itself to the shape of your body.

Oz: So what have we learnt so far, James?

James: Right. Barley is a grain that grows in a field. You harvest it and take it to the maltings. You moisten it and heat it up and fool it into thinking it's spring and the starch becomes sugar as the barley starts to grow little roots. And then you dry it in the kiln and that'll give you a pure malt that you would use to make a very pale ale or a lager. You can also heat it up more, which will caramelise some of the sugars, which means that it will produce less alcohol, because you need sugar for alcohol, but it will increase the flavour and colour, and that's how you would use it to make a very dark, rich beer.

Oz: Very good. There's also a special malt called crystal malt that gives British beer its characteristic flavour and dark, tawny colour – you can't get that colour from pale ale malt. As well as chocolate malts and dark malts, you can have roasted barleys – really bitter like badly burnt toast – all of these things give different flavours to the beer.

James: OK, assuming you've got your malt as you want it, the brewer buys it and he puts it in water and boils it up and the sugar is released, then he transfers the hot sweet liquid into another vat and shoves in ... the hops.

After all this information we need a bit of a lie down – in the malt.

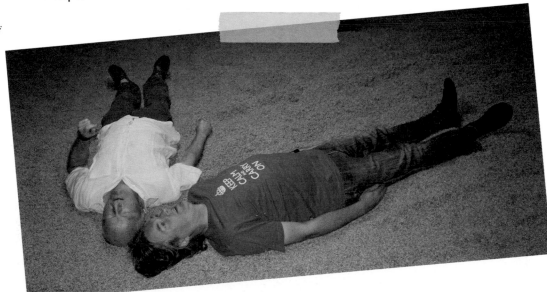

Oz: Ah yes, hops. Next stage of our journey takes us to Thornbridge brewery at Thornbridge Hall in Derbyshire. The brewery was set up in 2004, with the aim of creating great cask and bottled beers. Its India Pale Ale, Jaipur, has gained quite a reputation among beer lovers. Well, me, anyway. I don't live far from my local, but when it has Jaipur on tap I have great difficulty remembering how to get home. Anyway, hops.

A HISTORY LESSON *for fat heads*

Oz: The reason we've come to Thornbridge is to learn about the next vital ingredient of a good pint — hops.

James: What actually is a hop? Is it a fruit, or a vegetable?

Oz: The hop is a sort of weed, related to cannabis of all things, and it would sprawl all over the place if you let it, so it's cultivated on hop poles. Now, for thousands of years British beer, or ale as it was then known, was made without hops. The ale tasted sickly and cloying on its own, and so all sorts of herbs and spices were added to give it a bit of bite or attack.

It was Dutch traders who brought hops to England — they preferred their beer to be 'bitter' tasting, and that flavour comes from the oils and resins in the hop when it is boiled.

At first there was a lot of resistance — from the nobles and monasteries who owned the rights to the herbs and spices that were added to ale, but also from the people — there were uprisings about hops!

But eventually the fact that hops made beer more refreshing, and also made it last longer, won people over.

24

James: Made it last longer?

Oz: Ales didn't last long because they didn't contain much to protect them from bacteria in the air, so beer turned sour pretty quickly. The hop plant is a very good antioxidant – you put hops into a beer and they stop it going off.

All the brewers realised that, with hops in, the beer would keep to the end of the barrel and they wouldn't have to throw half of it away. The antiseptic quality was important in the beginning, but the flavour was a wonderful bonus.

OZ'S

BEER FACT!

"Beer is like a soup. You make the soup out of barley and water, but it doesn't taste of very much until you start putting in extra flavours – that's where the hops come in. Hops are the utter joy of beer - the spices, the seasoning, the salt and pepper."

Everything that's great about Britain – the crunch of caravan wheels on the gravel drive leading up to the ancestral seat. It's enough to make you weep.

James: Caravans are not very hi-tech. They have a Meccano chassis and the bodywork is comprehensible to anyone who ever made a cardboard building for a train set.

Finally we meet the young brewers: Kelly, from New Zealand, and Stef, an Italian.

James: You see, there's a blow against your idea of smocked peasants toiling merrily in the fields – he's a Kiwi and he's an Italian. I like the idea that people from all over the world are coming together to make beer, because beer is the answer.

Oz: The point is that to recreate what we need to preserve in this country we need new blood – the mongrel approach.

27

Kelly and Stef claim to get paid in beer which, judging by the quality here, is no bad thing. In the glistening sunlight of a July afternoon, we try rubbing the hops, which are the female flowers of the hop plant, and this releases the oils – which smell of orange, ginger and numerous other spices.

Kelly tells us you might have up to 70 hop flowers in a heavily hopped pint of beer. At Thornbridge they use American, English and New Zealand hops.

Stef says they add hops in stages. First they add hops to the wort – the hot sweet soup of malt and water – and boil it to release the bitterness and the antioxidants, then more hops are added for flavour. Finally, with the beers at Thornbridge, they switch off the heating and add a huge amount of hops as the wort cools down, which really boosts the flavour and aroma.

Kelly explains that price of good hops for craft beers has gone up as much as 500 per cent in the past few years, due to catastrophic weather in hop-growing areas, which have lost crops to floods and typhoons. Another result of global warming is that when a farmer can get more money from biofuels than hop-growing, he's going to rip up his hops. Of course, the leap in price means he'll be replanting them just as fast.

Oz: What that means is not that brewers should stop using hops, but that people should be prepared to pay the right price for a good pint, because even with the massive hike in price, the average price of hops in a British pint is still less than a penny a pint. Craft brewers might pay twice as much – so if you like a hoppy beer, don't look to a 'national' brand.

Stef and Kelly have set up a table of ale for us to sample, in the picturesque grounds of Thornbridge Hall. We taste the beers, or rather James tastes the beers first, which means that Oz has to stay sober and drive.

James: I got the first drink in so you're driving the car and having the water.

Sorry!

In their Kipling beer – described as a 'South Pacific Pale Ale' – Thornbridge uses the amazingly aromatic Nelson Sauvin hop from New Zealand. That's a hop fact.

Oz, though somewhat annoyed at not being able to try the marvellous Jaipur India Pale Ale on its home ground, nevertheless offers a beer-tasting tip:

Oz's beer tasting tip:

➡ What you do to taste a beer is burp it back to get the flavours – that's the way you judge the hops in a beer.

After a couple of glasses, James is waxing lyrical:

James:

The sweetness is a nymph being chased by a Viking of bitterness down your gullet. The G spot of drinking is somewhere in your throat. If you spit it out it's an affront to Bacchus. I can't burp because it's like trying to go for a waz when someone's standing next to you. I can't burp on demand – I can't burp the alphabet.

Oz: The faster the glasses go down, the better James's descriptive powers become.

HOP

FACTS!

Oz:

Dry-hopping means adding hops after the wort has cooled and the beer has fermented – this adds hop aroma but no bitterness. Boiling gets all the bitterness out of the hops, but then you cool the beer down and throw in more hops. Because it's gone below boiling point the bitterness isn't extracted from these hops, but more aromatic oils gently dissolve in the beer. Dry-hopping is fantastically important! It produces heavenly aromas, but does leave a hop sediment in the cask that needs cleaning out.

James: They smell like beer.

INDIA PALE ALE

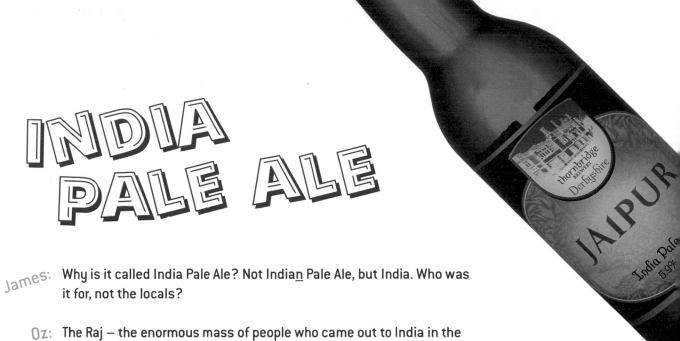

James: Why is it called India Pale Ale? Not India<u>n</u> Pale Ale, but India. Who was it for, not the locals?

Oz: The Raj – the enormous mass of people who came out to India in the heyday of the British Empire. Beer wasn't made in India, and if you tried to sail beer over the equator it often went bad. They used to hold auctions on the docks for any barrels which made it there without going off – prices went sky high.

But by adding loads of hops to the beer, and keeping the alcohol content relatively high, they overcame the problem and could happily send barrel after barrel to India. The intense hopping acted as an antiseptic and an antibacterial – even as you crossed the equator, the hops would be fighting the heat and infections, and keeping the beer fresh.

Finally James manages a **massive belch.**

Oz: What's the flavour in your mouth?

James: Beer

Oz: Why do I bother?

India-related James's ∧ notes

Raj fact: the pith helmet was designed as a test for malaria. You put it on, out in the tropics, and if you think you look good in the mirror, you've probably got malaria.

Elephant fact: Why do elephants drink? To forget.

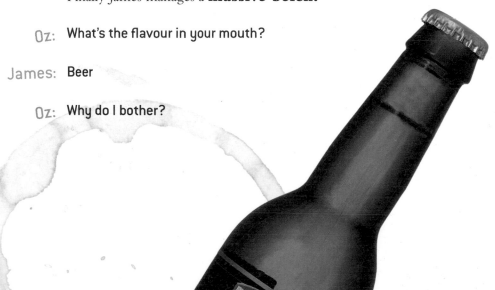

2

in search of an honest drink

Ship Inn Brewery, Low Newton by the Sea
So close to the sea, the beer even tastes of it

George Bowden, Leventhorpe Vineyard
Don't laugh – it's a real vineyard in Yorkshire

Patsy Slevin, Prospect Brewery
If Patsy's isn't an honest pint, nothing is

West Riding Refreshment Rooms, Dewsbury

King's Head, Huddersfield

Stalybridge Station Buffet Bar

RAIL ALE TRAIL

CHAPTER 2: IN SEARCH OF AN HONEST DRINK

'there's trub in't mill'

So we've learnt a bit about beer, but now we want to try to find an 'honest' drink. What's that, you may ask? Well, it is a drink that isn't pretending to be something it's not. A drink that does what it says it'll do on the glass, bottle or, if you must, tin. In this age of multinational corporations spinning us a line about every mediocre brew they come up with, **we want to find some people who make something that they are proud of – something into which they put some of their passion and knowledge**.

Unsurprisingly, where you find an honest drink, you'll find an honest brewer, pub or winemaker. And you'll find all three 'oop North'.

SATNAV:

TECHNOLOGY OF THE TOILET ROLL

Oz: Does SatNav do things like common sense? No. It's the buffoon's map for people who have a complete lack of interest in where they're going, and a complete lack of originality as to how to get there.

James: To some extent I agree with you – it's like looking at a map through a bog roll. But it's a useful supplement to the map – it just tells you where to go.

Oz: I've no idea where we are, James, except it must be the North because there's loads of blue sky and it's bloody freezing.

James: If you think that thing sits on the dashboard making an annoying noise, you should try sitting here with you in that seat.

Our first stop is in Standish, near Wigan. We're going to learn a bit more about how you make beer, and if ever there was an honest woman brewing an honest pint it's Patsy Slevin.

We pull up outside an ordinary house, in an unremarkable street. Straight away we can smell something unsuburban and interesting. It must be a brewing day. We find Patsy in her 'microbrewery', which is a garage big enough for one 'reasonably priced family car' squeezed in at the side of her mother-in-law's house. She makes six beers in here.

WHAT'S BREWING?
(HOW TO BREW AN HONEST PINT)

Oz: Patsy, we've been finding out about beer, and how it's made. Can you explain what you do here?

Patsy: Well, we're nearly at the start of the process and I've got 180 gallons of wort in this container.

James: When you say 'wort', that's the malted barley with the water?

Patsy: That's the sweet water, yes.

Oz: Sweet water? That's a much better way of putting it than than 'wort'. I thought brewers never used the word 'water'?

Patsy: No, they don't, they say cold or hot liquor, but 'wort' is sweet water – that's exactly what it is.

Oz: That's what I mean about honest.

The hot liquor and malted barley are put into a big vessel, called a mash tun. It's left to stand for about an hour and a half, and then the liquid is run off and more hot liquor is added to the grains to flush out any remaining sugar. This is called sparging the wort (from the French *esparger*, to sprinkle, if you're interested). This mixture is then pumped into a stainless steel vessel (called a copper because it used to be made out of copper) where the hops are added and the mixture is boiled.

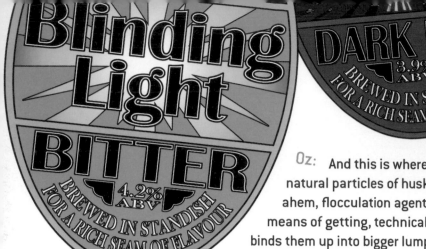

Oz: And this is where the trub rears its ugly head: the small natural particles of husks and hops and whatever. You add a, ahem, flocculation agent to remove the 'trub'. Flocculation is a means of getting, technically speaking, floaty bits out of a liquid. It binds them up into bigger lumps that drop to the bottom of the vessel.

There's no alcohol yet; that happens when the yeast is added – which you do next, after cooling the hopped mixture down and transferring it to a fermentation vessel. Fermentation usually takes four or five days. Once the yeast has done its work, it remains in the beer. This could make the beer cloudy, so brewers add a fining agent to clarify it. Egg white is sometimes used as a fining agent in winemaking. Patsy uses isinglass.

Patsy: The only thing we put into our beer, when we put it into the casks, is isinglass finings to clear the yeast to the bottom and stop the beer being cloudy. Because we now drink out of glasses instead of pots, people want clear beer. Isinglass is made of fish's swim bladders. Sturgeon were originally used, but now other fish are used, too. Thousands of years ago people used the stomachs of animals and swim bladders of fish to carry liquids. They found that when they put their wine or beer into a fish's swim bladder it was clearer when they got to their destination than if they'd used a sheep's or goat's stomach.

38

Honest beer requires honest hard work. James uses Oz's love of all things traditional to make him clean the yeast out of the fermenting vessel.

Honest and dishonest beer

James: What makes your beer particularly honest?

Patsy: It's got no fancy technology used to make it, it isn't artificially faffed about with – it's just malt, water, hops and yeast, with the isinglass added at the end.

James: So what's a dishonest beer?

Patsy: A lot of beer drunk in pubs is kegged beer – not cask-conditioned beer. I add a little bit of yeast to my casks to cause what they call secondary fermentation. This gives my beer a little natural head and helps condition it. But a lot of the keg beers are messed with – they have chemicals put in them, they're pasteurised and artificially carbonated. If you're a landlord, you've got to know how to look after cask beer – breathe the cask, reseal it every night. The beer will go off within three days if you don't look after it.

James: So the problem with proper cask beer – as opposed to the neutralised industrial stuff – is that it doesn't matter how good you are at making the beer, if the landlord's a numpty, it'll taste rubbish.

Patsy: Yes. Luckily for me I know everyone I deliver beer to – you build a relationship with them. But there are landlords who I won't sell beer to.

James: So one of the threats to proper beer is that a lot of landlords are not the type of people who necessarily love or even like beer and know how to look after it – they might be Australian, for example, and know the square root of diddly about proper beer as opposed to fizzy lager; so that's ruinous, isn't it?

Patsy: Aye, it is.

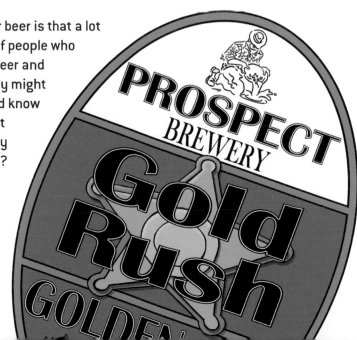

Oz's stint in the microbrewery has extreme odour and laundry consequences.

While Oz is doing honest hard work, James decides that it is not quite honest that they simply taste other people's wares, they should attempt to put what they're learning into practice; he suggests a Caravan Brewing Competition.

James: Oz, we can't just passively drink all this stuff — well we can, but it's hardly British — we should brew our own beer and submit it to independent adjudication to see who is the better brewer. Agreed?

Oz: OK — you use your new-fangled fancy ways and I'll brew proper beer the way it has been made for centuries, using good English equipment and English ingredients. Let's see who can produce a proper honest pint.

From now on James sleeps on the floor and Oz camps on the dining table. The so-called sleeping quarters — in a Sprite? Hah! — are now taken up by a mobile brewery, trub'n'all.

For the results of Oz and James's homebrew contest, turn to page 123.

KEGS, CASKS, BARRELS ETC

Casks and coopers

1 A cooper makes and mends casks or barrels.

2 'Cask' is the term used to describe any piece of 'cooperage' with a bulge in the middle, i.e. a barrel shape.

3 In brewing terms, a barrel is actually a particular size of cask, one holding 36 gallons.

4 Coopers would start their apprenticeship in the cooperage at the age of fourteen, and it would last for four or five years.

5 In the first half of the 20th century, there were around 600 coopers in the British beer industry. Now there are probably fewer than 20. Metal casks have widely replaced wooden ones, though all whisky producers and a few breweries still use oak casks.

6 Casks – for whisky, beer and wine – were made from oak, because as a new wood it adds sweet vanilla flavour and when aged it gives the liquid stored within a roundness or softness through gentle oxidation or 'breathing'. Other woods like pine would impart an unpleasant pungency.

7 Wooden casks are still hand-made, taking about eight hours for a skilled cooper, because no machine has yet been able to reproduce the qualities of a hand-crafted cask.

O'z's cask fact: a barrel is 4 firkins = 36 gallons = 288 pints

James's barrel fact:
The original coopered wooden barrel is the shape it is because it was designed to be handled by one person. You can knock it over, roll it, then tip it up again. If it was a flat-sided cylinder, you would never be able to pick it up once it was on its side – that's a barrel fact.

James's beer container fact:

People talk about cask beer and keg beer. A cask and a keg look almost the same – like a metal barrel – but it's a cask if it simply has beer in it at atmospheric pressure with its own yeast working away; it's a keg if the beer is under pressure with carbon dioxide in it and other additives which make it come out cold and foamy.

YORKSHIREMAN MAKES WINE!

Shock! Horror!

We go in search of another honest drink.

George Bowden has been making wine for God knows how long (and He would know, because He's a Yorkshireman). In Yorkshire. **Where real men drink beer.**

Oz: We're entering what one might call the 'côtes de Castleford', where the warm air from Castleford's industry floats up the valley and warms George's vineyards at Leventhorpe. What's more, his vineyard is in a rain shadow from the Pennines, so all the rain from Lancashire magically passes over his vineyard and goes on to dump on the rest of Yorkshire.

ON THE YORKSHIRENESS OF YORKSHIRE WINE

A handy old gibbet at the corner of George's field was the ideal place to 'hang' his vineyard sign.

Oz: Yorkshire is God's own county and a Yorkshireman can do anything he wants to do.

James: I know, but a Yorkshireman shouldn't want to make wine – it's not a very Yorkshire thing, it's not manly, industrial, decent – it's wrong.

Oz: George's wine used to have a strong mineral quality, but it was more the mineral of a rusting steelworks than of a Chablis. But the last couple of times I've had it, to my amazement, I thought it was pretty good.

James uses the knowledge Oz has passed on to him to assess George's placement of the vineyard.

James: He's got it on a slope, and it faces the sun, and the soil is quite infertile, so the vine struggles and its roots go deep and that increases its hardiness. The hardiness of the vine makes the grape struggle to ripen but that gives it more flavour, especially if he does a green harvest, which means cutting off immature bunches to reduce yield. I'm just showing you I've been listening.

Oz: (patting James on the shoulder) You have, and if you were a real person I'd say well done.

James: If you were a real person you wouldn't keep touching me like that.

George explains that vines have been planted in Yorkshire for 2000 years. Romans grew vines here. The only time there were no vines here was between World War I and the 1980s – and that's when he came along. Among other varieties, he grows Madeleine Angevine grapes, which ripen in 70 to 80 days; they are ideal for these conditions as they ripen early and are usually harvested from mid-September on into October.

43

THE TERROIR!!!

James: I can't believe I'm asking this, but what's the terroir like in Yorkshire?

George: This particular terroir is first class for the grape varieties we grow. Sunny, sheltered, with light sandy soil that drains very quickly and allows for early ripening. All the sunshine in the world won't give you a good wine by itself; it's the warmth, too. Location, location, location – and I chose this one specially. I was driving past here after it had been snowing and this was the only field in the area free of snow – the snow melted immediately, indicating that it was a field that retained warmth. It's called the Charlemagne effect because the Holy Roman Emperor used to tell his vine growers to plant where snow melted first.

Oz: Did Charlemagne get to Yorkshire?

George: No. But if he had... What's interesting and helpful to us English wine producers is that the consumers who turned away from French wines to New World wines are now turning back to wines of more delicacy and lighter alcohol. That's exactly what we make here. It can be profitable, too. If you plant about 5 or 6 acres and do everything yourself, from growing the vines to making the wine, it's about as profitable as having 400 acres of cereals. The input is about the same – one's intensive, the other's extensive.

Oz: So when you get vine-growing right in Britain, it's a very profitable operation.

George: You've got to make sure you have a decent crop every year – 3 tons an acre on average – for a good standard of living. You get about 800–850 bottles a ton.

Oz: Or 13–14,000 bottles a year if you've got 5 or 6 acres.

George: Hm. Well, last year we only got about a third of that, but it evens out. The first ton pays for processing, the second ton pays for bottling and the last ton gives you the profit. Although we're so far north, I haven't had to reduce yield to let the grapes ripen – this little vineyard keeps the heat up: it can be 40 degrees plus here on a good hot day. The soil dries and goes white, reflecting the heat up to the canopies – which are there to stop the heat escaping. The heat builds up during the day and rises up the hill to the top of the vineyard. The spacing of the vines is important too: if they were any wider apart, the heat would probably escape.

> LEVENTHORPE SEYVAL 2005 TASTING NOTES
> James: Well, my olfactory glands give me one word: 'buttery'.
> Oz: It's fairly neutral, a touch of Chablis, Bramley cooking apples, sage, strange Yorkshire herbs. George, this is by far the fruitiest wine I've tasted of yours. What's that down to?
> George: It'll be the vines.
> James: Fathead.

WINE AND GLOBAL WARMING

Scotland is planting a vineyard. And, according to Britain's top vineyard geologist, this is just the beginning. In fact in 75 years' time, at the present rate of global warming, **we'll be sipping sophisticated, delicate white wines grown on the sunny slopes of Loch Ness**. If someone had suggested to Oz two or three years ago that even Yorkshire was capable of producing a glass of wine that had the flavour of anything but coal dust and drizzle, he'd have laughed. But now Leventhorpe Vineyard near Leeds has made something that not only tastes like wine, it tastes like good wine. Is nothing sacred?

Global warming is changing the wine map of the northern hemisphere. In the short term this means that we in **the UK may hit a viticulture gold mine** as the climate enables us to produce the classic grape varieties of Burgundy: Pinot Noir and Chardonnay. Indeed it is even conceivable that we will outstrip our French cousins as their classic regions become too hot to carry on producing the world-famous varieties. Just imagine, Côtes de Castleford 2075 may become the finest vintage of the century. In the long term, of course, the consequences are not so pleasing: seasons change and that most important element of viticulture, predictable weather patterns, becomes a distant memory. Wine itself will start to change.

righteous ale

chicken

organic wine

I'm worried that because beer is the drink of people who make things, and we don't make things any more, our taste for different beers may go too. We've gone from a nation of empire builders, bridge builders and engineers to people who mince around worrying whether chickens are happy – and who will start drinking organic wine.

It's a Saturday, somewhere in Yorkshire, and James is thinking some dark thoughts. You can tell – bubbles are coming out of his head.

THE HONEST PUB

We've found two honest people making two honest drinks. We now go in search of an honest place to drink in. It's all very well to have good local beer but if your pub is pants then it affects the whole experience. A good local requires a good landlord who knows how to look after the beer. We decide that a good place to experience a few honest pubs in one go is on something called the Rail Ale Trail.

The Trans-Pennine Rail Ale Trail is a Yorkshire–Cheshire institution. A series of station bars are linked by a train and you can taste up to 30 beers on the way. We start at the bar in Dewsbury. Oz is in raptures about the West Riding Refreshment Rooms: **'It's what a station bar should be like'**.

Ten years ago it was just a waiting room; then father and daughter Mike Field and Sarah Barnes decided to turn it into a pub. It's an honest pub – run by people who love beer and like people drinking it. They're not worried about 'customer turnover' or 'average spend'. They like to have people in their pub being jovial, happy and a bit tilted. **That is an honest pub**.

The Rail Ale Trail: Stalybridge Station Buffet and some of the array of ales at the King's Head in Huddersfield.

James: Beer is not aspirational like wine is; there's a lot of pretension in wine. I admit I've come to enjoy wine greatly since I met you, and I drink it a lot and do appreciate it, but there's an aspirational quality to wine, a social one-upmanship about being able to talk about it and pretending that you've been to France. Beer is an honest drink – you drink beer because you like beer and you can't really be a beer snob because it doesn't attach itself to any social snobbery, it is simply beer. It's a drink for people who are thirsty.

Oz: I agree, up to a point. After all, Britain is a beer-drinking nation. We have also become a wine-drinking nation in the past 20 years, but most of that has been about aspiration. People do drink wine because they think it's posh. Even posh people drink wine because they think it's posh. But people drink beer because they like it. What I want is to make sure they get an honest, interesting pint.

James: It's beer – it's something I have a craving for at the end of the day.

Inevitably this leads to a rant about the big breweries – the reason so many people love the Rail Ale Trail is that it is honest. The big breweries are trying to make beer less interesting, they're trying to make it into a commodity rather than something anyone cares about. James introduces the CAMRA issue into the conversation. He admires what CAMRA are trying to do, even if they are a bit beardy, bits-of-bird's-nest-in-jumper kind of people who drink from acorn cups. The fact that they take their beer seriously is good – what he doesn't want and what he's wary of, though, is any attempt to intellectualise beer in the same way that the marketing people have 'intellectualised' crisps; so 'Oak-aged Tuscan Balsamic with a hint of Cornish Sea Salt' is simply a way of charging £2 for salt and vinegar crisps.

We assess our attitudes to proper crisps rather than the fancy, existential 'flavours' beloved of marketing men in suits and ties. This is the Honest Crisp Flavours league table as judged by James May and Oz Clarke (from the telly).

crisp league table	James	Oz
Flavour	1	2
Roast Chicken	4	1
Plain (Ready Salted)	3	4
Roast Beef	2	6
Salt and Vinegar	5	3
Cheese and Onion	6	5
Smoky Bacon	7	7
Prawn Cocktail		

Soup of the day (vegetable)

Steak and kidney pie
Succulent chunks of steak and kidney
drizzled with mouth-watering gravy,
presented in an individual earthenware
dish and topped with puff pastry

Sausage and chips
Two prime pork sausages, served with chips

Vegetable selection
A selection of vegetables. From the country
kitchen garden

Beer and minerals
Beer
Minerals

A range of waters

James's

↖ SNAPPY
GUIDE TO
PUB FOOD

The way to judge food in a
pub: if it's got a big menu,
be suspicious; if they bring
the food and it's in a
bowl – leave. That means
it's a gastropub and
they're being pretentious,
and they should be in
prison or breaking rocks.
It's wrong.

↖ Six real-life examples of landlords trying
to intellectualise the 'bill of fayre' and
making themselves look a bit stupid.

We thought honest drinks might be tricky to track down in corporate
Britain. But Patsy and George and Mike and Sarah are certainly an
inspiration – they show that honesty in what you do can pay dividends.
As we travel around looking for the drink that best represents the nation,
these people give us heart. We push on north to try to find more.

The Ship Inn at Low Newton by the Sea is
what we call honest: an honest northern
pub run by honest people serving
honest beer and honest local food and
patronised, in this instance, by a couple
of honest-to-God southern jessies. →

NEWTON BAY £22.50
LOBSTER
STRAIGHT OUT OF THE BAY - SERV
FRESH & LOCAL !!!!!!!
PLEASE ORDER IN ADVANCE AT T
(EVENING MEAL
ONLY!

SAND CASTLES AT DAWN

SEA COAL

SHIP HOP ALE

3

Scotland, or why Robbie Burns couldn't spell

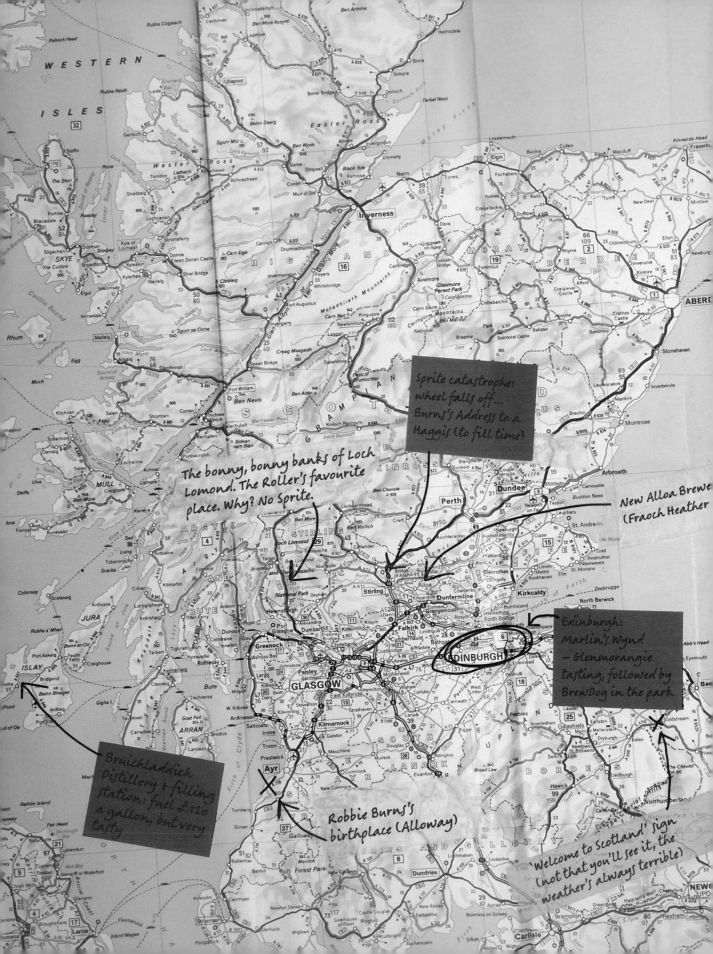

Sprite catastrophe:
wheel falls off...
Burns's Address to a
Haggis (to fill time)

The bonny, bonny banks of Loch
Lomond. The Roller's favourite
place. Why? No Sprite.

New Alloa Brewe
(Fraoch Heather

Edinburgh:
Marlin's Wynd
– Glenmorangie
tasting, followed by
BrewDog in the park

Bruichladdich
Distillery + filling
station: fuel £120
a gallon, but very
tasty

Robbie Burns's
birthplace (Alloway)

Welcome to Scotland' sign
(not that you'll see it, the
weather's always terrible)

CHAPTER 3: SCOTLAND, OR WHY ROBBIE BURNS COULDN'T SPELL

We cross our northern border in driving rain – in fact it's raining so hard that we can't see the 'Welcome to Scotland' sign. Or perhaps there isn't one? We drive on regardless, the SatNav artfully taking us on a three-times tour of Edinburgh before we reach our first Scottish destination, an 18th-century cellar called Marlin's Wynd. Apparently the serial killers Burke and Hare used to ply their grizzly trade in the streets behind the cellar.

WISH YOU WERE HERE!

Even when blindfolded, James can tell the difference between Rachel and Oz, using only his nose.

Marlin's Wynd is an appropriately dark

and broody location to be introduced to the pleasures of Scotland's national drink. The dominatrix Rachel Barrie, Master Blender for Glenmorangie, blindfolds us as a way of checking our olfactory prowess. We calm down when she explains what this means: **70–80% of the experience of drinking whisky is had through the nose**, so in order to increase the sensitivity of your nose, you remove one of the other senses – your sight.

Oz: This may prove tricky for James, who prefers that 90–100% of his drinking experience is through the mouth.

Rachel sprays six scents under our experienced noses. She explains that the technical term for the tasting process is a 'retro-olfactory' experience – effectively breathing the aromas of whisky out through your nose after you imbibe. We get mint, orange peel, lemon peel, vanilla, cinnamon and roses. Using taller stills to make the whisky is supposed to allow these subtle flavours to emerge.

Oz: I often use lemon peel to add to soups and stews.

James: You constantly talk about your culinary idiosyncrasies but do you realise that in all the time we've known each other, you have never even cooked me an omelette?

Oz: That's French. Why would I cook you that? You wouldn't eat it.

The serious business of tasting begins. Blindfolds removed, Oz and James's eyes light up at the bottles before them. Rachel pours decent measures into special tasting glasses and encourages them to 'swirl'. James's whisky barely reaches the bottom of the glass before he gains his first retro-olfactory experience. And then another. And then one more.

Oz: Here we are, being shown how to taste one of the most sophisticated drinks in the world – according to Rachel it has 143 different smells – and you're knocking it back like it's a pint of Stella.

James: It's a drink. I can only get about four of those smells.

Oz: That's probably because you're tipping it down your throat like the world supply's going to run out. There are at least six that I can get.

We add water to the whisky to release more of the flavour and smell. Water reacts with the spirit by breaking down some of the larger molecules, which in turn adds to the number of scents you encounter in the drink. Moving on to older and different styles of whiskies, James decides to take control of the tasting measures, pouring

Olfactory fact: Orange and lemon are two of the most desirable scents in the world; the most desirable is vanilla. Apparently it has associations with mother's milk.

orange

✓ *v. good*

lemon

✓ *v. good*

vanilla ✓ *excellent!*

himself and Rachel 'healthy' measures (although it is debatable how healthy quadruples are), but Oz gets a dribble in the bottom of his glass. Oz complains vociferously but is ignored by James, who is taking the tasting seriously. Very seriously.

James: **Most drinks are there to take you away from reflection and self-doubt; whisky, though, smells introspective. I associate it with philosophical moments in the dead of night. Beer makes you creative and energetic, wine makes you mellow and soporific, but whisky has demons in it: you can taste the slavering mad dogs that pursue you. It's a contemplative and introverted drink.**

Whisky is a complex drink – the language around it is much more sophisticated than that of beer and the drink itself rewards serious study, as James has shown.

We stagger off, contemplating whisky's complexity, and bump into two tramps in the park swigging beer from brown paper bags.

The tramps, it turns out, run Scotland's biggest independent mega-microbrewery ... phew. James Watt and Martin Dickie decided that microbreweries were all completely missing the point by marketing their brews in the cardigan and beard tradition of real ale. Instead they decided to take a much brasher, youthful approach and market to an audience they knew wanted interesting beer presented in an edgier way. BrewDog was born and, despite a faltering start, is now expanding very rapidly – particularly overseas.

The beers are given unusual names (Speed Ball, Paradox, Punk IPA, Hop Rocker) and made from unusual ingredients: guarana, kola nuts, Scottish heather honey and California poppy in the case of Speed Ball. The taste is deeply unusual and very exciting.

We get stuck in for some serious park bench tasting,

emerging only after having cracked open a very special Paradox brew that was matured in a 1968 Islay whisky cask to give it an intense flavour and an extraordinary 10% alcohol content. It is a mere £40 a bottle – and we're not talking a big bottle here. The copy on the label tries to explain their philosophy but they have recently fallen foul of the Portman Group (the drink industry's self-regulatory body – run by representatives from the big brewers), which had censored Martin and James for their advertising. **In particular, they objected to Punk IPA being described as an 'aggressive' beer**, claiming that this would encourage people to be aggressive. Those suits don't get it. This is a small-volume, high-quality beer described as having an aggressive flavour; like a pungent flavour – what, it'll stop people washing? – or a spanking fresh flavour – what, deodorize before you spank? – or an orgasmic...no, let's not go there. The suits said that the term 'aggressive' was in breach of the Code of Practice on the Naming, Packaging and Promotion of Alcoholic Drinks.

Oz and James agree – for once – on this issue: it's bollocks. There are major social issues with over-use of alcohol at their core. The alcoholic drinks concerned are generally made by the large companies and advertised in cynically suggestive ways. I doubt if Punk IPA will make even a single student drop his trousers in public, let alone attack a Belisha beacon with intent.

Oz's marginal old Scottish fact: *Edinburgh used to be known as 'Auld Reekie' — not because it stank to high heaven of Scottishness, but because there were 16 breweries producing good local beer in the city. Now there is one.*

The BrewDogs worked their magic — the Scottish range of drinks needed some soaking up. What better way to end our first encounter with drinking culture north of the border than to experience some of the culinary specialities? And we're talking niche here. Deep-fried niche. Café Piccante — 'the Chippy that thinks it's a Club' — will batter anything.

We're on a cultural mission to try that world-famous Scottish invention, the deep-fried Mars Bar. James notices that there are other potential victims to be sacrificed to the DEEP FAT FRIER and personally dunks a posh lolly into the holy batter before transferring it to the oil for exactly 2 mins 35 seconds. A Scottish feast of *deep-fried POSH lolly and Mars Bar on a bed of chips* is duly served up. It's washed down with the traditional bottle of Irn Bru — the not-so-soft drink.

I have to say that this is one of the very few things that I genuinely cannot eat.

The integrity of the Mars Bar has been disturbed or, rather, corrupted by the residual flavour of haddock in the oil. I got a deep-fried black pudding while you were doing the posh lolly — that's the real deal. Wonderful. The haddock residual actually improves it.

Our stomachs groaning with the fat, the grease and the deep-fried Scottishness of it all, we heave our bodies into the Rolls. Our next port of call is Alloa. But the SatNav decided to point us in the direction of Calais ('No, Alloa, fathead, not 'Allo 'Allo'). On the way we managed to find Scotland's most famous haggis shop – where the haggi roam free – and catch a stunning example of the species. We squeezed it into the van and headed for Calais, or Alloa.

At the New Alloa Brewery they make Fraoch (heather) ale from an ancient recipe discovered by the Williams brothers (Bruce and Scott) in 1986. It was written in a form of Gaelic comprehensible to only one person – a 92-year-old woman residing on Scotland's most westerly isle. With her dying words (**'then drink til ye fall o'er'**) ringing in their ears but the recipe

hoppy golden ale

porter with ginger root

heather ale

meadowsweet and elderflower

elderflower and lemon zest

safely translated, the brothers set about re-establishing the production of this ancient brew – it is said that it was first brewed around 2000 BC – after the tradition had lapsed earlier in the 20th century. They now produce over 1 million bottles of beer a year, using ingredients like meadowsweet, elderflower, heather, sweet gale and – James's favourite – pine needles.

We sit on the moors above the brewery and sip these flavoursome ales – they really do reflect the terroir.

pine needle beer (James's favourite)

elderberry beer

gooseberry beer

62

A SPRITE 78 CATASTROPHE

From one exceptional tasting experience

to another. We tap Islay into ScotNav and set off, caravan in tow. We rumble down the track and hear a rather odd noise, ignore it, carry on driving, but just as we are about to join the busy A9, we hear it again. We decide to check the caravan. James reverses the car to give us more space to work in. **There is an ominous shearing noise**, a thud and the next thing we see is a perfect example of a 1978 caravan wheel rolling serenely away from the van. **Our caravan — or cara-vin as Oz likes to call it — is knackered**. A bearing has bust and we have to find a new one. Helpful farmers appear from nowhere and set about trying to fix the poor Sprite 78.

Oz decides that this is **the perfect time to cook the haggis** and we settle down for a fine Scottish feast. At a slightly odd angle as the caravan is propped up not entirely on the level. We decide while eating that 1978 was a crap year for caravans — the manufacturers had clearly lost their bearings.

Oz: Haggis tastes wonderful with tomato ketchup and a quarter pint of whisky poured all over. When you're thirsty you can sup the whisky with a spoon.

James: No, the best haggis taste combination is salad cream and frozen peas and carrots. This makes it much more English.

ADDRESS TO A HAGGIS

Robert Burns

Fair fa' your honest, sonsie face, Great chieftain o the puddin'-race! Aboon them a' ye tak your place, Painch, tripe, or thairm: Weel are ye wordy of a grace As lang's my arm.

The groaning trencher there ye fill, Your hurdies like a distant hill, Your pin wad help to mend a mill In time o need, While thro your pores the dews distil Like amber bead.

His knife see rustic Labour dight, An cut you up wi ready slight, Trenching your gushing entrails bright, Like onie ditch; And then, O what a glorious sight, Warm-reekin, rich!

Then, horn for horn, they stretch an strive: Deil tak the hindmost, on they drive, Till a' their weel-swall'd kytes belyve Are bent like drums; The auld Guidman, maist like to rive, 'Bethankit' hums.

Is there that owre his French ragout, Or olio that wad staw a sow, Or fricassee wad mak her spew Wi perfect sconner, Looks down wi sneering, scornfu view On sic a dinner?

Poor devil! see him owre his trash, As feckless as a wither'd rash, His spindle shank a guid whip-lash, His nieve a nit: Thro bloody flood or field to dash, O how unfit!

But mark the Rustic, haggis-fed, The trembling earth resounds his tread, Clap in his walie nieve a blade, He'll make it whissle; An legs an arms, an heads will sned, Like taps o thrissle.

Ye Pow'rs, wha mak mankind your care, And dish them out their bill o fare, Auld Scotland wants nae skinking ware That jaups in luggies: But, if ye wish her gratefu prayer, Gie her a Haggis!

The James translation: Something to the effect of having need of a haggis ... the haggis is large ... it has gushing entrails and a sonsie face.

That's it, all the rest is illiterate rubbish.

With no bearings to be found, we have to abandon the caravan. We feel sad about leaving it behind – but mainly because it's got all the beer in it and someone could steal it. The Rolls, however, loves it - free at last of its naff encumbrance, our luxury conveyance glides around Loch Lomond, caressing the road and gambolling with the energy of a spring lamb. We relish the freedom too – this is the proper use of the Rolls and we fight to see who can drive for a change. **There is also the advantage that we can stay in a hotel and get a decent night's sleep**.

OF ISLAY MALT, QUADRUPLE-DISTILLED SPIRIT AND APPELLATION CONTRÔLÉE WHISKY

Whisky fact:
malted barley, water and yeast are the basic ingredients of whisky. Add some oak barrel aging, and that's it.

Islay is beautiful when the sun is out but can be bleak and windswept when it isn't. It's utterly gorgeous when we drive off the ferry. Needless to say, word of our arrival spreads rapidly and a storm hurtles in from Ireland bringing all the lambent moisture of the Atlantic.

There are apparently **two things that really distinguish Islay malts from other whiskies in Scotland: the sea and peat**. The sea is a particular factor at the Bruichladdich distillery (our ultimate destination on the island) because they mature the whisky in sherry casks on the island; the sea air from the ocean only yards away permeates the casks, giving the whisky a real flavour of Islay. The heavy peating of the whisky is born of necessity: there are very few trees or other fuels on the island, and at one time the whole process was fuelled by peat. The water here is particularly pure and all of the distilleries on the island have their own source of spring water.

Islay malt is famous around the world – and not only because it makes one quarter of the Scotch that is exported. It is also the most characterful of Scottish whiskies. In fact, some say that it *is* the personality of Scotch whisky, because even a non-Islay whisky that has any personality usually has Islay blended in.

Speed, bonny boat, like a bird on the wing ... over the sea to Islay.

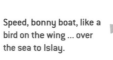
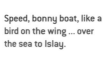

WHISKY

HOW IT'S MADE

It's actually beer without the hops, until you start distilling it

You basically start with small beer. To get that, you malt barley – which means germinating it, letting it develop for a bit so that the starch in the grain turns to sugar. The germination is then stopped by heating the barley (traditionally on Islay this was done using peat fires, which imparted the smoky smell and taste to the whisky). The barley is then ground to create a 'grist', which is a kind of coarse flour. The grist is 'mashed' – the process is simply one of mixing it with hot water. This mash turns into a wort, which is a sweet malty liquid – the solid part is drained off and used as cattle feed.

Yeast is then added to the wort and the fermentation process begins. The point of the fermentation is to convert sugar into alcohol. Distillers are not that choosy about which yeast they use, unlike brewers, who can be fanatical about their yeast. After between two and four days the wort becomes a sort of beer (called a wash), about 7% alcohol by volume.

The next bit is the clever bit. An ancient Arabian alchemist was trying to make eye shadow – called *al kuhl*. He took a black powder, liquefied it, vaporised it, and allowed it to solidify again into a very delicate black eye shadow – which we still call kohl. It's possible that he then thought, sod it, this is thirsty work, I'll drink the next batch. Next thing he knew, he had a traffic cone in his room and a sore head. Well, someone had to be first.

Now, where were we? So the wash is distilled two, three or (if you want to make rocket fuel) four times. The first distillation increases the strength to about 25% alcohol by volume. The second distillation makes a far stronger spirit, about 70% alcohol, but it is only the middle part of the distillation – the heart, they call it – that is pure ethanol. (Ethanol is the good type of alcohol; methanol and others are bad alcohols, nasty-tasting and sometimes dangerous to health.) The early part of the distillate is called 'foreshots' and is pretty pungent stuff that would harm the whisky's flavour. The late part of the distillate is 'feints': oily, increasingly pungent, and again, although a little of the 'feints' adds character, a lot spoils the whisky. Only the 'heart', the 'new make', the central cut of the distillation run is used to make whisky. The spirit is then usually diluted – ideally with the same water the whisky is made from – down to 63.5% and then matured in oak casks for a minimum of three years, but in the case of the great single malt whiskies, this will be anywhere from eight to 20 years.

Blended whiskies – the big brand names such as Famous Grouse, Bell's and Johnnie Walker – are a mix of true malt whisky and big-volume industrially produced grain whiskies (using grain other than malted barley). Single malts are never blended with any other whisky.

In this giant and ancient flailing machine, the grist is mixed with water to create the wort, which will become the wash after fermentation and then spirit after distillation. Only after it's been in a barrel for at least three years does it become 'whisky'.

One of the reasons Islay's distilleries became popular in the old days was because of the advent of blended whisky in the mid-19th century. Big whisky-makers in Glasgow and Edinburgh began to produce whiskies largely made up of grain whisky – cheaper than malt whisky and made from unmalted grains such as corn and wheat – mixed with a smaller amount of malt whisky. As grain whisky has a relatively neutral flavour, the distillers prized highly characterful malts, such as those from Islay, to give 'personality' to their blends. To this day, Islay whiskies are sought after by whisky blenders for the intensity of their character.

Everything at the Bruichladdich distillery is very old: the buildings, the stills, the barrels, the grist mills, the methods, the beliefs and the jokes.

James: So when you're given one of those whiskies and it tastes like a grow bag, it has probably come from Islay?

Oz: You have to be smart, don't you? These Islay whiskies tend to be smoky, bearded, beetle-browed; they're standing out against the roaring tempests of the winter. They're great big bearded hooligans in kilts.

James: So all whiskies are sorts of warriors? They're claymore-wielding, hairy-arsed Scots troublemakers?

Oz: They are that; but with Islay malts you get all of that and in the middle of it all, in the middle of the storm and fire and fury, when you swallow you realise that there at the absolute heart of the whisky is a beautiful sweetness, a richness of fruit and a lovely malty softness – even if it's covered in beard and fur and fungus.

After a night swapping stories with the locals in the bar **we arrive at the Bruichladdich distillery**. James immediately spots a Radical sports car. Unable to restrain himself he finds out that it is powered by whisky. Yes, three bottles of quadruple-distilled spirit are enough for him to take it for a spin.

James:

Whisky is a spirit and is produced by a process known as distillation. In the early days of the motor car, petrol was known as motor spirit and it is also produced by a process of distillation. It therefore follows that whisky must be a fuel and, more specifically, it must be a biofuel because it's made with grain.

Now what I have here is some Islay spirit. This stuff has been four times distilled for extra strength, and its strength is now roughly the same as unleaded petrol. I'm told that if we put this into the fuel tank of this Radical racing car, then we can drive it up and down the road on whisky. By putting this in the tank it makes the car officially drunk — this is a whisky-powered car!

However, that stuff works out at about £120 a gallon, so the moral of this story is, put petrol in your car and drink Scotch whisky. And that's a whisky consumer advice fact.

The owner of the distillery, Mark Reynier (who like Oz is 'displaced', but in his case from Belgravia, not from a palace in Harrow, or Ireland, or wherever Oz is actually from), explains that 60% of the barley they use is organic Scottish barley, so they know exactly where it's from.

Oz's whisky facts:
1. A single malt is made only from malted barley and distilled at a single distillery. That's the actual definition.

2. Age statements (10, 12, 18 years etc) refer to how long the youngest whisky in the bottle has matured in cask. The longer the whisky has spent in a cask, the more the wood will affect the flavour and colour of the whisky.

Running a racing car on Scotch whisky is a fairly pointless, not to say excruciatingly expensive, exercise. But the exhaust fumes do give the spectators a bit of a buzz.

THE TERROIR!!! OF WHISKY!

James and I have explored every highway and byway of what terroir means in wine production, but in the case of whisky, there is much discussion in the whisky-producing world about what effect terroir has on Scotland's national drink. The problem is that it is by no means clear which elements that go into making a fine whisky are influenced by where they are grown or situated. The exception to this is the water, which no one disputes has a huge effect on the final taste of the spirit and, of course, is fantastically important when you use it to reduce the cask-strength whisky to the normal bottling strength of 40–46% alcohol by volume. But there is a raging debate about whether local barley makes a big difference and whether the shape and size of the still is a vital ingredient. I'm inclined to say 'yes' to both ideas.

Some suggest that instead of using an imprecise French word like terroir to describe the less tangible influences on whisky production, we should embrace the idea of what contributes to the 'soul' of a whisky. The idea that a drink has a soul gets my romantic taste buds

tingling. And as we look out towards the glowering Islay skyline, and think of the ancient sods of weather-worn peat, the fury of the furnace flames and the tumult of the fermentation and distillation, followed by the long years – winter, summer, winter, summer again – that the whisky rests and broods and waits in these low, dark barns, the idea of the 'soul' of a whisky starts to make absolute sense.

An intensive tasting session follows in which we need to check, re-check and triple check that the many different whiskies on offer are up to scratch. As we swirl, sniff and swallow we ask ourselves why there isn't an appellation contrôlée for whisky – it would make perfect sense to guarantee a minimum quality for whisky to protect its global reputation. But how low – or high – would the distillers set that minimum quality? Further down the bottle a flash of inspiration brings literary insight: Robbie Burns's spelling was so bad because he drank so much of this stuff.

Our next stop is a place – a country, a nation, no less – that is defined by just one drink…

Everything shown on these pages can affect the flavour of the finished whisky: the sea, the sky, the wood of the barrel and the amount of cobblers being talked in the tasting room. That's terroir.

4

Two pints of Oirishness, to be sure

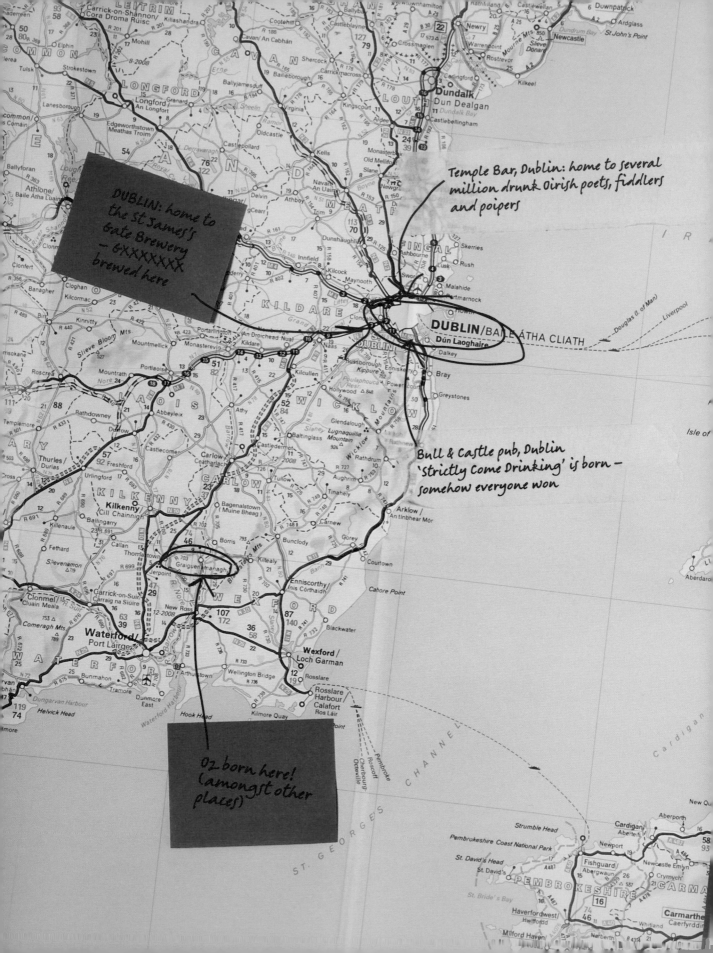

DUBLIN: home to the St James's Gate Brewery — 6xxxxxxx brewed here

Temple Bar, Dublin: home to several million drunk Oirish poets, fiddlers and poipers

Bull & Castle pub, Dublin 'strictly Come Drinking' is born — somehow everyone won

O₂ born here! (amongst other places)

CHAPTER 4: TWO PINTS OF OIRISHNESS, TO BE SURE

'A pint of plain is your only man'
Flann O'Brien

Leaving our slowly fermenting beer

in the stricken 'cara-vin', we hop over to Dublin.

James: Since when has Ireland been in Britain, Oz?

Oz: OK, not for a bit, but we're coming to Ireland because if we're in search of a drink that defines a nation, here we have the ultimate example. And, as we're here, it's worth our while having a taste of the Irish real ale scene, which is starting to flourish.

There is one drink that made Ireland and Irishness famous. It's debatable whether there is a drink in the world that is more synonymous with a country than G******* (note to reader: for BBC 'compliance reasons' we're not at liberty to mention which dark stout ale brewed in Dublin since 1759 we are going to taste. Apparently it might give it 'undue prominence'). We make a bet that whoever mentions the G word owes the other a fiver.
Pure genius.

We find the 250-year-old brewery founded by Arthur G with the aid of Sean (the Irish voice on the SatNav) and are met by Fergal Murray, the famous Irish stout's Master Brewer.

Fergal Murray is the man responsible for the worldwide taste of the G drink – and that means over 4 million pints a day. At different times in its history the site has been the largest brewery in Europe and, after World War I, the largest in the world. At its peak more than 4000 people worked on the site and the general feeling was that quite a few of them never bothered to go home. Well, why would you?

BREWING STOUT

Irish stout traditionally follows the same process as ale brewing, **but the addition of roasted barley to the wort gives stout its black colour and burnt toast bitterness**. Traditionally they roast the barley for three hours; during the last 15 minutes the temperature of the grains reaches 450°C and they acquire the dark colour and toasted flavour we associate with true Irish stouts. Nowadays the drink is pasteurised, supposedly to 'remove the micro-organisms that can affect the taste over a couple of weeks in the barrel'. In fact it's just to ensure that even if your pint is served by a halfwit with a palate of lead, it'll basically taste the same as that served by a skilled, caring publican.

The barley is roasted, and then before you know it you're talking in a silly accent.

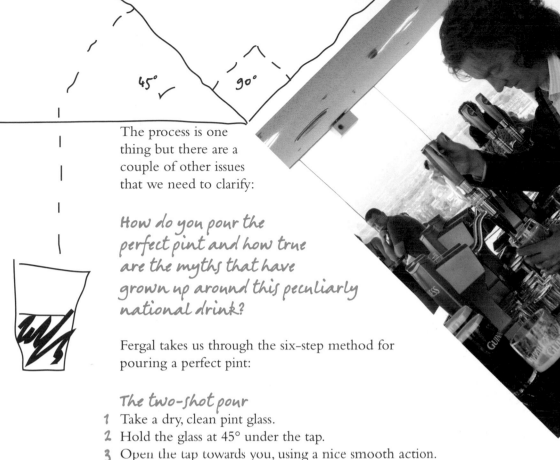

The process is one thing but there are a couple of other issues that we need to clarify:

How do you pour the perfect pint and how true are the myths that have grown up around this peculiarly national drink?

Fergal takes us through the six-step method for pouring a perfect pint:

The two-shot pour

1 Take a dry, clean pint glass.
2 Hold the glass at 45° under the tap.
3 Open the tap towards you, using a nice smooth action.
   When the beer reaches the bottom of the harp symbol on the glass (Whoops. Too much of a clue. It could be any symbol – pickaxe, cocker spaniel, euphonium), slowly straighten the glass to the perpendicular. When the drink reaches the top of the harp – or pickaxe, cocker spaniel, euphonium – stop pouring.
4 Rest the pint until the bubbles have all accumulated into the head; they will surge and then settle as the head builds up.
5 Now push the tap away from you (this makes the pour slower) until the head sits slightly proud of the glass.
6 Present the pint to the customer.

Notes:

Don't trace silly shapes of male genitalia in the head. It's not funny. A shamrock's bad enough.

According to Fergal, you drink through the head, leaving the head on top of the pint down to the last drop.

The critical 45° angle

Fathead fact: It takes 119.5 seconds to pour the perfect pint of stout. There is, apparently, even a stance that is recommended for drinking this perfect pint. James throws himself into the posture (back straight, elbow at 90° to the shoulder, faraway look in the eyes).

THE MYTHOLOGY OF ~~GUINNESS~~ GOODNESS

A number of myths have grown up around this dark brew – including the idea that it is good for you because it contains Vitamin G. As, of course, there is no such thing as vitamin G, this is another piece of Oirish humour.

1) It's made from Liffey water.

It may have been at one stage but, if you look at the Liffey now, you'd be glad it no longer is.

2) It's good for you.

This was a slogan dreamt up by the advertising company S H Benson in the 1920s. Based, very scientifically, on asking people how they felt after they had drunk a pint. Apparently the answer was frequently 'It makes me feel good.' How other brewers must have wished they'd asked the question first. There is iron in the drink and it was given to blood donors after they'd done their duty, as a means of replacing some of the lost iron. It is still marketed as being 'good for you' in some countries, but advertising standards killjoys have now forbidden this in the UK and the USA.

3) It tastes different in Ireland.

Well, we're at the headquarters of the brew – surely this is the place where you'd get the ultimate pint? Not necessarily. Allegedly there is a secret 'essence' which is transported to each of the 49 breweries around the world and added to the local ingredients to make the taste as standard as possible. But the best pint could as easily be found in, say, Nigeria (the second biggest consumer in the world) as in Malaysia. Indeed Bono (Oz: 'who?') swears by the Jamaican version. But has he tried the Nigerian version which, they say, 'has a baby in every bottle'? (Not literally, obviously.)

4) Alcoholics Anonymous in Dublin is across the road from the brewery.

Apparently not, but in the non-corporate days of yore, employees were given an allowance and could be given a 'bonus' of a large bottle for work above and beyond the call of duty. No wonder it was considered 'prestigious' to work there.

PORTER AND STOUT

what's it all about?

In the 18th century dark, full-bodied porter was the most widely drunk beer in Britain. There was no real difference between it and stout porter, double stout or triple stout, except the strength. **The name 'porter' comes from the drink's popularity with the street-market porters of London.** The 'stout' aspect related to its strength. The G drink was originally called 'Extra Superior Porter'.

One of the reasons for Irish stout's peculiarly dark colour and bitterness compared to the British version is that malt was particularly heavily taxed in the 18th and 19th centuries, so **instead of using just malted barley in the brewing process Arthur G and his contemporaries roasted some barley as well.** They saved money and gained a competitive advantage in the export trade over their British rivals. This also helped boost the popularity of Irish stout worldwide.

During World War I, to save energy to use for the war effort, the British Government barred British brewers from roasting the barley. However, they did not impose the same restrictions on Irish brewers – quite rightly they were scared of the effect on an already rebellious Irish public, what with 1916 and all that. So while dark porter and stout styles became almost invisible in England, Scotland and Wales, in Ireland they took hold and flourished. Ireland managed to vastly increase her exports of stout, and **the extraordinary link between a drink and a nation was forged.**

We decide to find out what happens when you walk into an Irish pub and ask for 'a pint'. Do you get 'a pint of what, sir?' or does the barman whip out a glass with a harp on it and start performing the two-shot pour? **We head towards an area of Dublin called Temple Bar**, which is where a particular 'brand' of Ireland is marketed very intensively and where you'll see more people flat on their faces than at a carpet-staring competition for the short-sighted. This is stag and hen party hell. The landlord responds with the two-shot pour.

We emerge from the pub to discuss Irishness. James has a theory which has been brewing almost as long as Guinstuff itself.

IRISH v OIRISH

James: If you look around, there are actually two kinds of Irishness: ordinary Irish and Oirish. Oirish is what the marketing men of the country would have you believe: it's the fake Gaelic writing, the 'craic', the Liffey water and all that rubbish; Oirishness is a marketing exercise to sell a picture of a country that doesn't exist. And it's the most successful Irish export after the G drink. It's this idea that when you walk into a pub the bloke looking misty-eyed in the corner is a poet or a novelist or a folk musician — when actually he's just one of the many local drunks. It's the idea that after 10.30 (when the Americans have gone to bed) all the locals get their violins (sorry, fiddles), drums and pipes out and have a spiffing good sing-song until the early hours. It's all rubbish.

Oz: But it isn't all rubbish, James. I am after all a native son of the Emerald Isle.

James: A what? Just where are you from, Oz?

Oz: From Graiguenamanagh, you know, down south a bit.

James: So. Let's recap: you're from Scotland, Yorkshire, Kent and the North-East. A man of everywhere and a man of nowhere.

Oz: I'm a man of the British Isles and I belong everywhere.

James: You're a raving berk of the British Isles. You're from everywhere, so you belong nowhere.

Oz: Anyway, you're wrong about Oirishness. Irish is real and what you see happens in every pub in every village in this beautiful land.

James is unconvinced, so Oz takes him to his 'home' town for a few pints. You can hardly hear yourself think over the noise of a terrible cliché.

We decide that there is one beer question that needs resolving:

which is better for your hair, lager or stout?

For this scientifically controlled experiment we decide that James's luxuriant growth will be the guinea pig, as it were. The process is that the hair is washed 'normally' and then the beer used as a conditioner – half of the head covered in stout, the other in lager. The result is clear – the hair that has been 'stouted' dries to a softer, fuller, more lustrous condition than the side that has been 'lagered'. Indeed the lagered side is brittle and dried out; imagine what it does to your insides if that's what it does to your hair. Still, if your hair is too full and soft, just use lager as a conditioner and you'll end up looking like a squirrel.

A NOTE ABOUT IRISH WHISKEY

It seems remarkable now, but at the end of the 19th century and in the first part of the 20th, Irish whiskey was more widely drunk in Britain and the USA than the Scotch variety – and was more highly thought of. However, Prohibition cost Irish whiskey its American market, and after Irish independence it lost sales throughout the British Empire.

Like the famous stout brewers – and again, originally for economic reasons rather than out of a preference for one taste over another – most Irish distillers use a mix of malted and unmalted barley. The result is a richer and oilier whiskey than Scotch, with a rounder, fruitier flavour.

Pure pot still whisky is unique to Ireland. Once the backbone of Irish distilling, it is made in batches using triple distillation, and it is a key component in many Irish whiskey blends. There are very few pure pot still whiskey bottlings available.

The hair experiment over, the kind people from the local Carlow brewery suggest that we go to the Bull and Castle pub in Dublin to sample some of the huge variety of craft beers being made in Ireland at the moment. **We arrive at the Bull and Castle, where there are over 70 different bottled beers available and 15 types on tap.** The names of the brews and the variety of styles reflect the recent surge in craft beermaking in Ireland. If you asked for 'a pint' here you'd certainly be asked 'what of?'. As it happens, there are 11 craft brewers in the pub that night and we decide to have a small tasting competition – and as this is television we invent a game show:

STRICTLY COME DRINKING

James: Hello and welcome to Strictly Come Drinking

Oz: We're in the fair city of Dublin in Oireland

James: We've got a group of Irish craft brewers together

Oz: And they've each brought along a sample of their beer

James: We're going to give them 15 seconds to tell us why their beer is truly Irish

Oz: And we're giving them points for their points (OK, pints. I thought it was a good joke)

James: And points for their blarney

Oz:
James: In the meantime, keeeeeep drinking...

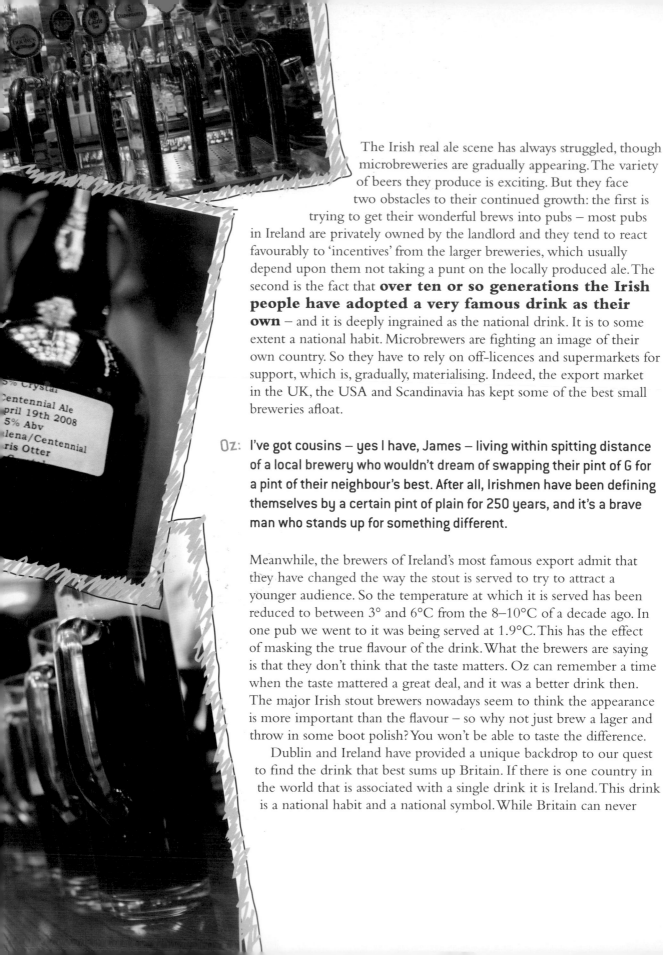

The Irish real ale scene has always struggled, though microbreweries are gradually appearing. The variety of beers they produce is exciting. But they face two obstacles to their continued growth: the first is trying to get their wonderful brews into pubs – most pubs in Ireland are privately owned by the landlord and they tend to react favourably to 'incentives' from the larger breweries, which usually depend upon them not taking a punt on the locally produced ale. The second is the fact that **over ten or so generations the Irish people have adopted a very famous drink as their own** – and it is deeply ingrained as the national drink. It is to some extent a national habit. Microbrewers are fighting an image of their own country. So they have to rely on off-licences and supermarkets for support, which is, gradually, materialising. Indeed, the export market in the UK, the USA and Scandinavia has kept some of the best small breweries afloat.

Oz: I've got cousins – yes I have, James – living within spitting distance of a local brewery who wouldn't dream of swapping their pint of G for a pint of their neighbour's best. After all, Irishmen have been defining themselves by a certain pint of plain for 250 years, and it's a brave man who stands up for something different.

Meanwhile, the brewers of Ireland's most famous export admit that they have changed the way the stout is served to try to attract a younger audience. So the temperature at which it is served has been reduced to between 3° and 6°C from the 8–10°C of a decade ago. In one pub we went to it was being served at 1.9°C. This has the effect of masking the true flavour of the drink. What the brewers are saying is that they don't think that the taste matters. Oz can remember a time when the taste mattered a great deal, and it was a better drink then. The major Irish stout brewers nowadays seem to think the appearance is more important than the flavour – so why not just brew a lager and throw in some boot polish? You won't be able to taste the difference.

Dublin and Ireland have provided a unique backdrop to our quest to find the drink that best sums up Britain. If there is one country in the world that is associated with a single drink it is Ireland. This drink is a national habit and a national symbol. While Britain can never claim to have one drink that could match up to this, it does provide a yardstick by which to measure the drinks that we do class as our own.

If a pint of plain isn't our only man, though, what is?

Next, we move to the traditional home of British beer, Burton-upon-Trent, to continue our quest. Phew. Neither of us owes the other a fiver.

LOCK-IN PUB GAMES

Played with pieces of paper and a pencil for people who know how to make their own entertainment.

IN THE HAT

Each person in the group tears a piece of paper into 20 strips and writes the name of a famous person from history on each one. These all go into the hat (or similar dry vessel), folded up.

Players split into teams of two

At each team's turn, one member pulls names from the hat and tries to prompt the other to guess as many as possible in a minute. For example:

Name pulled from hat: George V
Player one: 'Bugger Bognor!'
Player two: 'George V!'

Teams keep the names they guess correctly. The team with the largest collection of pieces of paper when they've all gone from the hat (or similar dry vessel) wins.

ON THE 'EAD

Each player writes, on a strip of paper and in such a way that the player to the left can't see it, a word or name relevant to an agreed theme: articles of clothing, actresses, vegetables, WWI fighter aces, etc.

Each player then sticks his or her strip on the forehead of the player to the left, so that it is visible to everyone else.

Each player in turn then asks questions of the group in an attempt to arrive at his or her identity. Questions must be such that they can only be answered 'yes' or 'no'. A 'yes' answer earns the privilege of another question; a 'no' means play moves to the next person.

Last one out is either a chump or some obscure division three winger from the 1950s.

5

Gone for a Burton

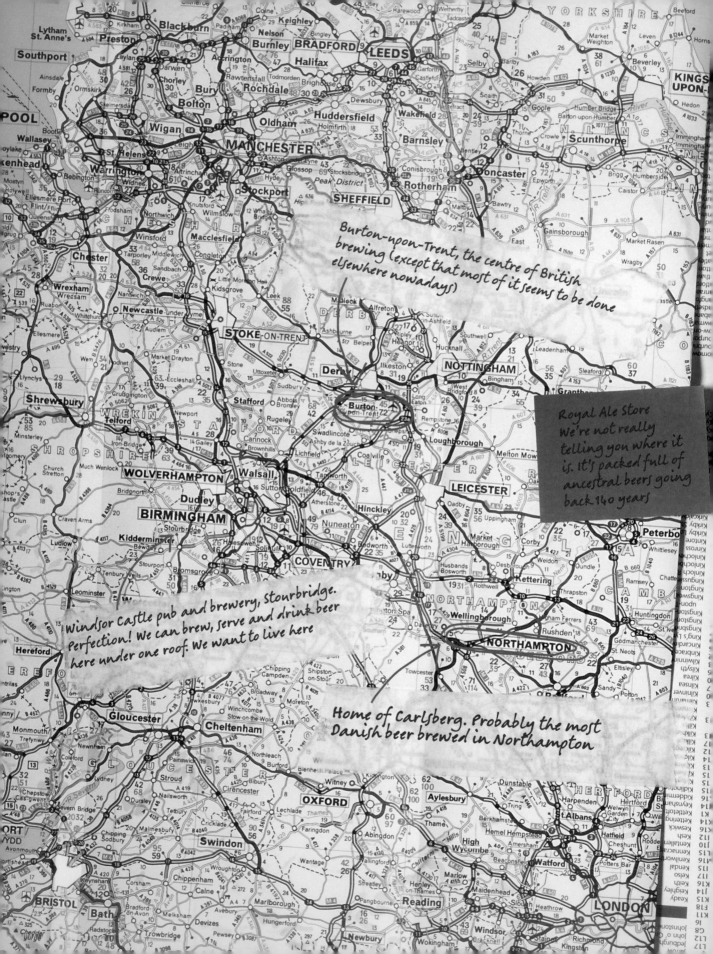

Burton-upon-Trent, the centre of British brewing (except that most of it seems to be done elsewhere nowadays)

Royal Ale Store
We're not really telling you where it is. It's packed full of ancestral beers going back 140 years

Windsor Castle pub and brewery, Stourbridge. Perfection! We can brew, serve and drink beer here under one roof. We want to live here

Home of Carlsberg. Probably the most Danish beer brewed in Northampton

CHAPTER 5:
GONE FOR A BURTON

From Ireland we head back to the peace and calm of the Midlands. Peace? Calm? The English summer welcomes us back with downpours, leaden skies and icy winds. The caravan has been mended – sort of – and **it sits surrounded by a pool of water in the hotel car park.** The roof leaks, we've discovered, which doesn't fill us with much confidence for the rest of the trip, although it does fill the caravan with quite a lot of water. Who needs California or the south of France when you can surf the M6 with a 30-year-old caravan?

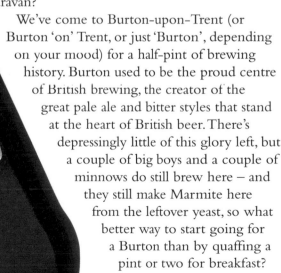

We've come to Burton-upon-Trent (or Burton 'on' Trent, or just 'Burton', depending on your mood) for a half-pint of brewing history. Burton used to be the proud centre of British brewing, the creator of the great pale ale and bitter styles that stand at the heart of British beer. There's depressingly little of this glory left, but a couple of big boys and a couple of minnows do still brew here – and they still make Marmite here from the leftover yeast, so what better way to start going for a Burton than by quaffing a pint or two for breakfast?

91

OZ'S BEER BREAKFAST

Throughout British history, people drank copious amounts of beer, from morning until night. Elizabeth I liked her beer, and drank a quart of ale for breakfast – and a quart of ale at that time might have been 8 or 9% alcohol.

James: Yes, but we now know she was a bloke.

Oz: Quite a lot of people not only drank ale for breakfast, but also drank a quart of wine. I mean, how were you supposed to operate machinery after that?

James: There wasn't any machinery.

Children weren't excluded, though they usually stuck with their two pints of breakfast ale. This went on for hundreds of years.

There were good reasons for this. First, beer contained nutrients and calories that might be hard to get from other foods, because of bad harvests or poverty. If you were doing a day's hard labour in the fields, you needed a supply of energy, as well as something that would quench your thirst. Beer fitted the bill perfectly, and workers might drink more than ten pints of beer a day to keep their hydration levels up, and their sense of the awful reality of their lives at bay.

Secondly, beer was safer than water. When you're making beer, you boil the water, and once you've boiled it, it's safe to drink. Before public sanitation, cholera, typhoid and other water-borne diseases were a real threat to health. So 'small beer' was brewed, often as a secondary, weaker, fermentation of a stronger brew, and given to all members of the household, including children and servants. So right up to the 19th century that meant that people thought beer was a perfectly natural thing to sup right through the day.

Oz's beer fact:
It only became illegal to sell beer to people under 14 years of age in 1901.

Legend has it that Saint Modwen lived in Burton for a while, before setting off to Rome around 700 AD. She started performing miraculous cures on people's eyesight using Burton water. A couple of hundred years later, Benedictine monks built Saint Modwen's Abbey in Burton to commemorate her good deeds. When monks get together they start brewing beer. Always. So this must have good claim to be one of the world's first breweries, started in 1002, and the Abbey's still there.

In those days monks had a terrific appetite for beer. The monks at Burton Abbey were given a daily allowance of 16 pints of ale: one gallon of strong ale, and one gallon of weak ale for those still standing. Or kneeling.

As brewing became more widespread in society, it was often women, known as 'ale-wives', who made the beer, brewing for their local communities as well as their families. The brewsters made celebration ales to mark special occasions. 'Bride ales' were brewed to celebrate marriages, and 'groaning ales' to mark the birth of a child, as well as working as an anaesthetic through labour, keeping the mother and midwife going, reviving the dad, anointing the babe's head…

Being pissed all the time didn't stop us ruling the world and inventing the steam engine. This is because we drank beer, not wine.

steam engine

the world: OURS
1800–1945 (approx)

Gradually commercial brewers took over. Scientific inventions like the steam engine allowed greater quantities of beer to be brewed more cheaply. Better roads, railways and seafaring allowed beer to be moved around and bigger companies to compete with, and eventually dominate, local brewers.

Oz: Now, we've already seen that hops made a huge difference to brewing, allowing beers to keep for long periods and making it possible to export beer in good condition to the far-flung corners of the British Empire, which made India Pale Ale a hugely popular style. It just so happens that the water in Burton was almost uniquely suited to creating this wonderful beer style, and here a little science lesson is in order.

WATER WORKS

The enormous number of wells that spring up all around Burton and the Trent are massively high in mineral salts. Burton water contains a lot of calcium sulphate and magnesium sulphate, which make it very hard, which is great for brewing pale and hoppy beers. The salts make the beer more astringent, and contribute to the bitterness of it, as well as pointing up the hop aromas and creating a bright, foaming, limpid beer. Lagers, for instance, are much softer beers, and need softer water. The waters at Pilsen in the Czech Republic, the birthplace of real lager, contain almost no salts at all.

'BURTON SNATCH'

Another Oz beer fact:
The characteristic sulphuric whiff of mineral salts in Burton beer became known as the 'Burton snatch'. If you're lucky enough to be drinking a pint with the Burton snatch, but want to get rid of the smell, drop an old penny in your beer. The copper will dissolve the sulphurous aroma. Don't use a new penny, though, as they don't contain as much copper, because the price of copper has gone through the roof in the past few years.

Oz: Anyway, back to Burton's history – and this is interesting, James.

James: Get on with it, then.

OK, OK. Now, I'm going to have to simplify this, but a couple of historical events coincided to turn Burton into the brewing capital of Great Britain. One was the development of transport links – **Burton's railway station opened in 1839** – which meant the town's brewers could distribute their beers far and wide, rather than having to rely on making a profit from a small local population.

Secondly, in 1845 the tax on glass was abolished and new beer glasses meant people could see what had been hidden from view in the old pewter tankards. **Sparkling pale ales looked nice** whereas dark porter looked like muddy oxtail soup. Pale ale became the favourite tipple of the emerging middle classes, and porter – formerly Britons' drink of choice – collapsed in popularity and was virtually extinct by the end of World War I.

Burton had always had a lot of breweries for its size, because the water was so suitable for beer, but now the demand for 'Burton Ale' turned Burton into a beer boomtown. In 1840 Burton's ten breweries produced around 70,000 barrels of ale per annum and employed approximately 350 workers. By Burton's heyday, in the late 1880s, there were 31 breweries, employing a total of 8,235 people and producing over 3,000,000 barrels of ale.

Bass – then the world's largest brewing company – employed 2,250 workers in Burton alone, and was bottling around 100 million bottles of beer per annum, reflecting the growing middle class demand for beer to drink at home.

'GONE FOR A BURTON'

This phrase was originally used in a series of adverts run by the town's largest brewery. In the 1930s the ales were so popular that a glass of beer was often known as 'a Burton'. The ads showed an empty chair at a dinner table, or a missing soldier in a parade, with the line: 'Gone for a Burton'. With typical gallows humour, the phrase was taken up by World War II airmen to describe colleagues missing or killed in action.

Things changed with refrigeration and other developments, which meant that Burton's achievements could be replicated elsewhere. **Breweries all over the country started producing beer using Burtonised water**, which is made by dissolving calcium and magnesium sulphates in the water.

More recently, the introduction of keg beers and then lagers changed the face of Burton for ever. **Now there are just a handful of brewers in Burton**, including the giant Coors plant, which makes keg lagers and beers, and Marston's, which, thank goodness, still makes a small amount of England's most famous beer, draught Bass.

But let's take a little break…

James: Oh, yes, please, let's.

Oz: And pay a visit to the Royal Ale Store, for a taste of brewing in Burton's pomp.

James: Now you're talking sense.

We hitch the caravan back on the Rolls and set off at a stately pace; Burton seems to have more speed cameras than anywhere else on the planet, **and that's a former brewing capital of Britain fact**. By a strange irony, the **Royal Ale Store** is buried deep in the heart of the Coors brewery, which seems to dominate Burton's landscape from whichever angle. We meet up with Steve Wellington, head brewer of Worthington's, which survives as a microbrewery, also on the Coors site. He's our guide to the Royal Ale Store. Steve explains that it was traditional in the old days that Bass brewed Royal Ales for many occasions, and that the Worthington Brewery is carrying on the tradition.

James: Royal beers are made in fairly small volumes for special Royal occasions – a Jubilee, the birth of a royal baby, Prince Charles passes his driving test, whatever – and they send some of them to the Royal personage, some of them are given to the staff as special gifts, and the rest stay on these racks; so they're celebration ales, but they're all something to do with the Royal family. Royal people may even have been involved in brewing an ale: the Queen came along, pressed a button, went home and they'd had to paint the whole place for the privilege.

Oz: The 1981 marriage of Prince Charles and Lady Diana was doomed from the start because their celebration ale was a lager.

A while ago Steve was investigating some remote areas of the brewery and he discovered some very old beers, including Ratcliff Ale, which was brewed in 1869 to mark the birth of one of the Ratcliff family – in those days the brewery was the Bass, Ratcliff and Gretton brewery. It's one of the oldest drinkable beers in the world – maybe the oldest – and valued at around £5000 a bottle. Steve opens one for us to taste.

TASTING 'PROBABLY THE OLDEST BEER IN THE WORLD'

£5000 and it still tastes shit.

James, shut your eyes and try and take yourself back 139 years.

James: OK, I'm swirling the beer and trying to think about all the things that have happened since this was incarcerated in the bottle.

Oz: It's like the gummy, solid bits on top of a bottle of tomato paste. This was brewed precisely halfway through Queen Victoria's reign.

James: There's an oily, dark sensation. It's what the walls of a Victorian prison would have tasted of if you had licked them. Strained through Magwitch's underpants.

Oz: I think it's getting fresher. A great drink, like an old Bordeaux, has one last hurrah – when it's hardly able to get out of the bottle – and this is its last hurrah.

James: If you uncork any Bordeaux just as Oz starts talking about it, by the time he stops it will have matured, if it hasn't evaporated first.

Oz: You're drinking it as if it was lager!

James: I couldn't drink lager like that. If I hold on to this for a while, my next wee will be worth £500. I'm not sure the essence of Victorian Britain agrees with me. Like Jerusalem artichoke soup.

We reflect on the changes that have occurred in British brewing in recent times, culminating in the domination of cheap, mass-produced lagers.

James: What we drink as a nation has set us apart from other European nations. They have the philosophers and café societies, and they drink wine and coffee. We're a nation of sweaty, inter-bred labourers and mass producers, and we drink beer and tea. Beer lets us have ideas, and tea gets the roads and the houses built. So it then follows that the most catastrophic change in the complexion of British society is our adoption of coffee and lager, because they don't suit the way the British people historically worked.

I like German beers and Czech beers but I dislike kegged, industrial, pub lagers because they're just beers for getting pissed with. They taste like antifreeze. It's a fundamental shift in the psychology of the nation – we no longer drink brown, food-like beer, we drink ice-cold, flavourless, headache-inducing lager.

Oz's lager fact: Lagers are fermented right out – so that all the malty richness and extra flavour and texture and things that were there before fermentation are gone and you just get more alcohol and less taste. You don't get the extra nutritious quality that the good old ales of England had.

The Devil's drinks

cappuccino

lager

Proud, upstanding, wholesome English ales, dreamt up by virtuous Midlands' brewers

OZ's LAGER HISTORY LESSON

In 1961, 99 per cent of the beer we brewed in Britain was ale or stout, and one per cent was lager. In 2006, 26 per cent was ale or stout and 74 per cent was lager. Eddie Taylor, the Canadian owner of Carling, was determined to switch Britain's drinking loyalties to keg lager. He did this by buying up breweries, and the pubs they owned, which in turn persuaded other brewers to consolidate and switch to keg lager and keg beer production, to try to stop him buying them up as well.

At first lager wasn't that successful, and even though there were lager pumps in all the pubs, nobody bought it. We didn't need to drink lagers; we had our own pale, bitter beer.

The arrival of TV advertising was the other nail in the coffin of real beer. Fifteen years of telling blokes they would be stronger, more handsome and sexier if they drank lager, eventually worked. By 1975 lager was so successful that part of the iconic Bass brewery in Burton was converted to produce 800,000 barrels of lager a year.

London businessmen and marketing departments, who had no contact with local drinkers, said, 'This is what beer should be – very modern. **It's in a keg, it will last six months, anyone can serve it, no cellar expertise is needed**. There were whole swathes of the country, like Northamptonshire and Norfolk, where you suddenly couldn't get cask-conditioned beers. The breweries were just after making the biggest profit; advertising and lack of choice – you'll drink what you're told to drink – put paid to cask beers and secured the domination of lager.

That's when the Campaign for Real Ale (CAMRA) came into the frame. They were faced with the complete destruction of the British beer tradition in about 20 years and that was all started by the bloke from Canada.

2662HL SHIFT VOL

Carlsberg is brewed at such an astonishing rate that a new tandoori restaurant has to open every five minutes in order to accommodate it.

As a passionate brewer, Steve Wellington at the Royal Ale Store had voiced optimism about the future of real beer, claiming that the market for mass-produced lager is now in decline as young people demand more taste in their drinks. James is of a more gloomy opinion…

James: In another couple of generations everyone will drink lager and no one will drink proper beer any more. Here we are in Burton, once Britain's brewing capital, and now it's all owned by lager brewers. Beer, as we like it, is doomed, because it no longer defines the nation. We're in search of a drink that defines modern Britain, and bitter or ale is no longer the drink that speaks for modern Britain because it's gradually turning into a craft-brewing thing, so it's for enthusiasts and connoisseurs, like canal boats and steam railways are.

Lager is the ruin of Britain because it's such an international drink. The problem with lager is it's meant to be cold and fizzy, and that idea came over with the Americans, who were trying to imitate the German beer they drank in Europe. America had refrigeration more widely earlier than we did: they developed a taste for cold fizzy things and we eventually followed. As we always do because we're a bit soft. We ended up as a nation of lager drinkers, which is a tragedy.

James's graph to express his and Oz's powers of erudition relative to beer consumption: Oz represents a steady incline, whereas James peaks early with a lengthy trail-off.

Steve argues that microbrewers are beginning to fill the void created when the big brewers stopped brewing cask ales. He points out that cask ale is actually more profitable than lager. We leave Burton with a glimmer of hope for the future of traditional British brewing.

James: The biggest threat to drinking is inoffensive beers. Gentlemen drink to contentment, not capacity.

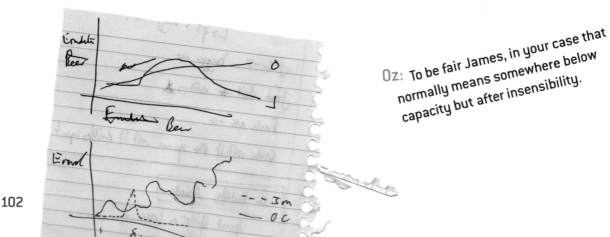

Oz: To be fair James, in your case that normally means somewhere below capacity but after insensibility.

All this pontificating leaves us thirsty and in need of a good night out. We pack up the caravan and head for the **Windsor Castle Inn** near Stourbridge, where we end up working for our drinks, though not very hard. Oz is confined to the cellar and James works behind the bar, if you can call drinking 'work'.

The Windsor Castle is an old-style pub, with old-style beers, but a pleasing, crisp white modern interior, and we're impressed by the range and quality of the beers made by Chris Sadler and his dad, John, who run the pub.

OZ'S WINDSOR CASTLE TASTING NOTES

The beers are all well made. I had the best mild I've had for a number of years: really proper West Midlands Black Country mild, a little bit stronger than a lot of milds, at 4 per cent – often milds are about 3.2 or 3.5 per cent. It was dry, blacker than Guinness, with a wonderful head on it – not just a pale white head, but a head you could see the darkness of the beer in – like a cappuccino with streaks of chocolate and toffee colour running through it. Milds are usually quite fruity, light and ruby brown. This one was black-brown and quite soft, and very tasty.

SADLER'S
"Incomparable" ALES
MILD ALE
BREWED BY SADLER'S ALES AT
THE WINDSOR CASTLE BREWERY
IN THE HEART
OF THE BLACK COUNTRY
4.0%

GOLDEN RULE OF THE PUB URINAL

There is only one rule of correct conduct at the pub urinal. Do not, under any circumstances, attempt to make a funny quip about better out than in, room for a small one, this is where the big knobs hang out, more than three shakes... or about the disturbing similarity between what you've just micturated and the stuff on sale behind the bar.

order of merit for
URINAL EXCELLENCE

Just have a waz, and then leave!

We leave refreshed and reinvigorated.

Britain needs more pubs like the Windsor Castle to try to turn around the fortunes of traditional British brewing.

Oz: Give the customers a choice of decent stuff over mindless rubbish and they will choose the good stuff.

James: Thank you for that commercial from Planet Oz. But we're doomed. Lager will win. Decent draught is dead. Fancy a pint of Black Country mild?

James's pub game rules – a guide to acceptability

YES ✓	NO ✗
Darts	Pool
Dominoes	Air hockey
Skittles	Quiz machine
Shove ha'penny	Safety darts
Scrabble	Space invaders
Chess	One-armed bandit
Draughts	Escape from Colditz
Backgammon	That stupid thing
Tic Tac Toe	with the dished
Pub quiz	tray and the dried
	beans, from Africa
	or something

6

If it grows, DRINK IT!

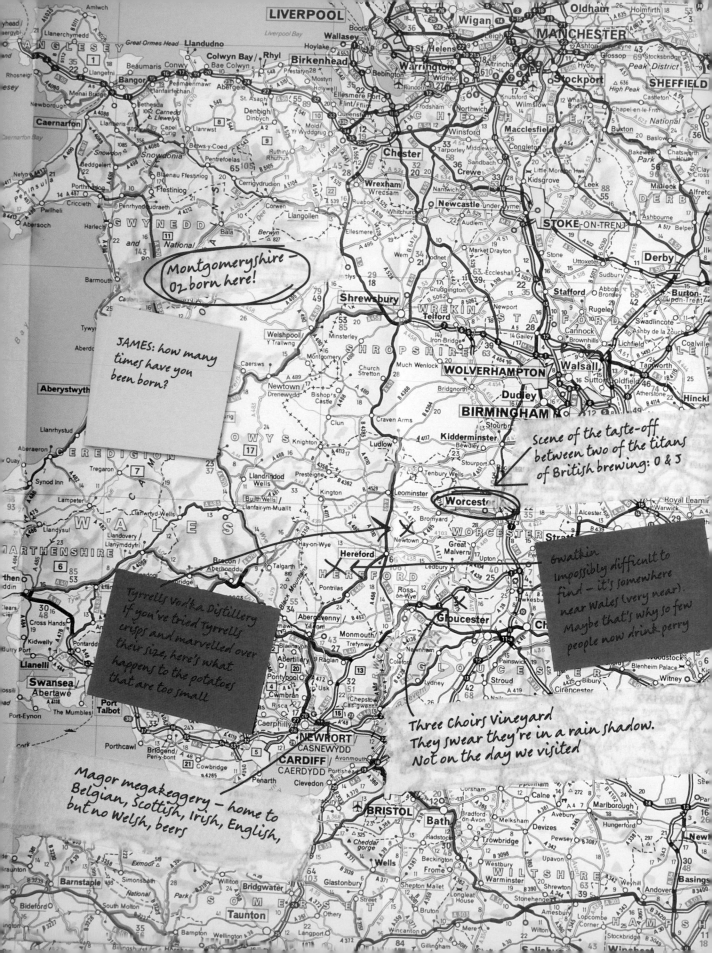

Montgomeryshire – O2 born here!

JAMES: how many times have you been born?

Scene of the taste-off between two of the titans of British brewing: O & J

Gwatkin impossibly difficult to find – it's somewhere near Wales (very near). Maybe that's why so few people now drink perry

Tyrrells Vodka Distillery If you've tried Tyrrells crisps and marvelled over their size, here's what happens to the potatoes that are too small

Three Choirs Vineyard They swear they're in a rain shadow. Not on the day we visited

Magor megakeggery – home to Belgian, Scottish, Irish, English, but no Welsh, beers

CHAPTER 6: IF IT GROWS, DRINK IT!

We bid the Midlands sweet farewell, and head over towards the sunny borders of England and Wales. Did we say sunny? More rain, more wind, more grey skies. What have we done wrong? Dear God, what have we done wrong? **We're used to wet weekends, ruined bank holidays, but an entire year soaked?** What *have* we poor Brits done wrong?

We're going to meet some brave, foolhardy souls who decided to make quality drinks from our national resources of good soil, no sun and buckets of rain. And they're actually doing it rather well, harnessing the best of British for a new take on some old favourites. They have looked our wonderful climate squarely in the eye and said, **'We don't care what you throw at us, we're going to make it anyway.'**

ARTISAN
POTATO VO
40% vol

Large shot!

(What James would call
a decent measure.)

POTATO VODKA

Our first stop is Tyrrells distillery

in Herefordshire. Tyrrells have gained a good
reputation for their handmade crisps, which are
aimed at the connoisseur end of the potato chip
market. What they're not particularly well known
for yet is their potato vodka. That's right, we said
vodka – in Herefordshire.

Vodka, a Slavic word meaning 'dear little water',
is an East European beverage, probably originating in
Russia or Poland in the 11th or 12th century but, as
with whisky, no one is absolutely sure.

Although an older drink than gin, vodka took
longer to become a staple of cocktails in the West.
The Russian revolution saw emigrants take their vodka
recipes abroad – to France and the USA. It was only
as recently as the 1960s and 70s that marketing and
consumer affluence conspired to make vodka a popular drink
in Britain. It now outsells all other spirits, including gin and whisky,
and 15 per cent of vodka produced in Britain is exported, including
to Russia.

Small-scale artisan production is still quite unusual though, and we
were intrigued to see how and why it worked. Most vodka is produced
from grain, but it can be produced from any starch-rich plant, including
Tyrrells' potatoes. But why would they produce vodka?
In Herefordshire?

Well, Will Chase (Mr Tyrrells) came across a vodka still while looking
for equipment for the potato chips. This set him off on a vodka voyage
of discovery, which culminated in the decision to turn some farm
buildings into Tyrrells' traditional batch distillery, rather than barn
conversions for holiday lets. Bad news for caravan owners, but good
news for British drinks connoisseurs.

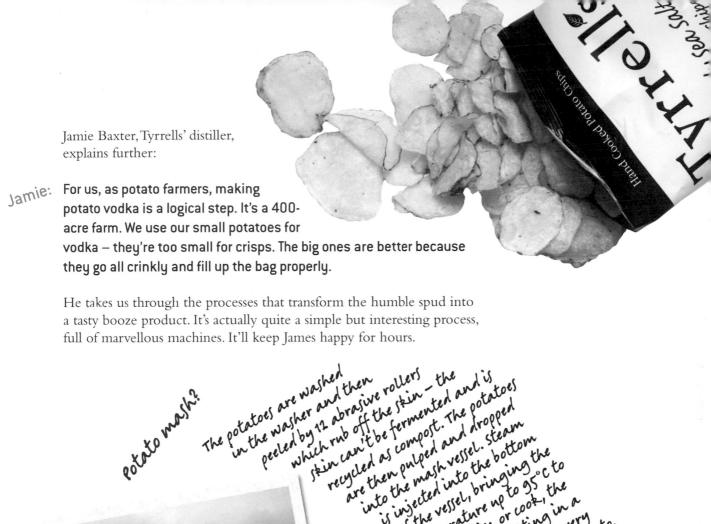

Jamie Baxter, Tyrrells' distiller,
explains further:

Jamie: For us, as potato farmers, making potato vodka is a logical step. It's a 400-acre farm. We use our small potatoes for vodka – they're too small for crisps. The big ones are better because they go all crinkly and fill up the bag properly.

He takes us through the processes that transform the humble spud into a tasty booze product. It's actually quite a simple but interesting process, full of marvellous machines. It'll keep James happy for hours.

potato mash?

The potatoes are washed in the washer and then peeled by 12 abrasive rollers which rub off the skin – the skin can't be fermented and is recycled as compost. The potatoes are then pulped and dropped into the mash vessel. Steam is injected into the bottom of the vessel, bringing the temperature up to 95°C to gelatinise, or cook, the starch, resulting in a potato slurry, a very runny mashed potato. (Tastes filthy, by the way.)

James: So at this point you *could* have it with cold ham, peas and parsley sauce. What you're saying is there comes a point in every potato's life when it has to decide whether to become mashed potato or vodka. What would you do if you were a potato, Oz? You almost are.

Oz: As an Irishman, I'm delighted to learn that a potato can have a choice.

The mixture is cooled to 60°C and enzymes are added to convert the gelatinised starch into sugar; in 20 or 30 minutes, it tastes sweet. The temperature is lowered again before the yeast is added, and then it's time for…

FERMENTATION

The purpose of fermentation is, of course, to produce alcohol, and after a week in the fermentation tanks they end up with a potato wine of about 8–10% alcohol by volume.

James: It tastes like the sick of someone who has got drunk on beer would taste.

Oz: And eaten a cheeseburger and a couple of portions of chips.

James: This must be the low point of the potato's soul, being turned into potato wine.

112

DISTILLATION

There's a batch still (a still that distils one batch at a time) with a small column on top of it. Next to it is the rectification column, which is about 50 feet tall. They are both 100 per cent copper and were hand made in Germany. To us they look a bit like they belong in the Chitty Chitty Bang Bang sweet factory, but Jamie says they've got soul, character, and the copper usefully acts as a catalyst and takes out some of the heavy metals. (What? From a potato?)

The first stage of distillation is called stripping: the 'potato wine' is gently heated in the batch still to extract all the alcohol. At the end of the stripping run they have a liquid that's about 50% alcohol by volume.

There are different kinds of alcohol, but they all vaporise at a lower temperature than water. Distillers talk about separating the 'hearts, head and tails'. They are looking to isolate the alcohol they want (hearts, or ethanol in scientific terms) from the other alcohols, which are harmful or unpleasant-tasting.

Oz's potato vodka fact: Higher starch potatoes produce more alcohol.

James's potato vodka fact: Mash can mean mash or it can mean mash.

Head and tails: the heads are methanol – you know, methylated spirits, loss of hair and sight, tastes terrible with Coke.

RECTIFYING

The impressive rectification column comes into play for the second and third distillation runs. Jamie explains:

Jamie: Rectifying the alcohol involves separating the methanol from the ethanol. Methanol is bad for you – it can cause blindness – so the fact it also tastes horrible is neither here nor there. Ethanol is the alcohol we want to keep, because it's the alcohol that tastes nice and doesn't kill you. Methanol is the smallest of the alcohols, it only has one carbon atom and therefore the lowest boiling point, which makes it rise all the way to the top of the column, where I trap it. So all the methanol comes through first, and we can take it out from the rest of the batch.

Shortly afterwards the ethanol, the heart, starts to come through and we collect that – it makes up about 80 per cent of the run – and then we get the higher alcohols coming through; again we separate those off. And we do all that by sniffing! Most vodka these days is made using computer-controlled stainless steel continuous stills.

The distillation produces the 96% alcohol pure spirit, which is diluted with water from the aquifers beneath the orchards on the farm. The water is purified, so it's neutral-tasting, and then used to blend down the alcohol. Vodka by law has to be at least 37.5% alcohol by volume. Decent vodkas, including Tyrrells, are 40% abv. All the flavours come from the potatoes that we've used: you can taste the character, it's like buttery mashed potato when you drink it!

James: Surely a vodka is just a vodka, like a crisp is just a crisp?

Oz: No James, this is what distinguishes small-scale artisan production from the big breweries! Care and attention. Every batch requires a hands-on approach to keep the character and consistency of the vodka.

We're about to find out about hands-on attention.

BOTTLING AND TASTING

Every bottle has to be filled by hand and the corks are hammered in individually with a small wooden hammer – the joys of small-scale, artisan production. Every batch sticker has the signature of the distiller (Jamie) on it. He compares this to getting lines at school, and considering they produce 3600 bottles a week that's quite a few detentions.

James: Given that you make a range of flavoured crisps, have you considered making a matching range of premium vodkas? Cheese and onion vodka, prawn cocktail vodka, smoky bacon vodka, ready-salted vodka?

Jamie: No.

James estimates that each bottle contains about 12 lb of potatoes. So vodka is very expensive in terms of lost crisps.

115

James has a go at bottling and labelling the vodka. It takes him 28 seconds to do one bottle, or 28 utterances of 'pass me the butter please', which is the way Oz counts it. James prefers the 'one elephant, two elephant' method of measuring a second. We try both ways. Over 10 seconds Oz is 1.2 seconds out, James is 1.3 seconds out. Butter wins.

We agree that the vodka is very pleasant — quite fruity.

Fortified by a drop of premium English vodka, we gather our wits and head off to taste what is perhaps one of the least well-known drinks still made in the British Isles – perry.

PEARS FOR YOUR HEIRS – THE PERRY STORY

Perry could claim to be one of the oldest drinks in Britain. Most perry drinkers claim that it is certainly older than cider, because the cider apple trees mainly came over from Normandy and Brittany after the Norman Conquest. But perry is still something of a mystery to us and to many others, so we went to see Denis Gwatkin, who makes some of the finest perry in the country. Denis is a heavy metal fan with a passion for pears. **His perry has won numerous awards including, confusingly, best cider, which prompts the question: What exactly is perry?** It turns out that it's quite simple really: it's like cider only made with pears. Well, not quite *that* simple.

There are special perry pears that can only be used to make perry. And you really wouldn't want to eat them – they're bitter, sharp and as hard as bullets. In style, perry is in between cider and wine – Denis's award-winning perry is about 7.5% alcohol by volume – only it tastes of pears, not apples or grapes. The process for making perry couldn't be simpler: you pick the pears in the autumn, mash them up, squeeze the juice out of the resulting pulp, chuck the juice in an old whisky barrel and let the natural yeasts on the skin of the pears and in the barnyard get to work to ferment the juice. Once the fermentation has stopped, you put a bung in the barrel and let it mature for three to four months at least, but not as long as cider. And Perry is your uncle and cider your maiden aunt.

So what's the difference between perry, pear cider and that 1970s' travesty Babycham?

Many of the perry pears have fantastic names, such as:
Brown Bess
Butt
Ducksbarn
Gin
Golden Balls
Green Horse
Harley Gum
Hellens Early
Hendre Huffcap
Honey Knob
Late Treacle
Merrylegs

Denis explains that pear cider (which is becoming increasingly popular) is basically cider with an essence of pear added – it has nothing really to do with perry. Babycham is another matter altogether: a sparkling pear cider that took the drinking world by storm in the 1960s and 70s, it was commonly mixed with brandy to make a, ahem, 'Legover'. It has gone through several revivals, but the idea of a drink marketed solely to women seems, well, very 1970s now.

Interest in perry has increased, but the very fact that it takes so long for the tree to grow, that the fruit doesn't last like cider apples do, and that it is perhaps even more subject to the vagaries of the weather, make perry production a hazardous business and certainly not one you can set up overnight. Gwatkins have been at it for ages, but until 1992 they just made a barrel or two for themselves and their friends. The commercial market barely existed. A chance entry to a beer festival, where they won the best 'cider' award – don't ask – transformed their fortunes and the Gwatkins now lead an expanding tribe of perry makers, saving – and building on – the perry tradition. We find ourselves on somewhat familiar territory if not on familiar terroir.

very old pear

02's
PERRY FACT

"It can take up to 50 years for a perry pear tree to start producing fruit – so you can't rush into production. Once it starts producing fruit, though, it can go on for 250–300 years. Hence the saying 'pears for your heirs'."

THREE CHOIRS

After what seems like weeks of beer, we're actually beginning to miss wine. So it's lucky that we're heading for the award-winning Three Choirs vineyard, deep in the picturesque Gloucestershire countryside. The rain lashes down, followed by a minute of sunshine before a tornado sets in again.

To James's astonishment, they're producing not only white wine, which suits cooler climates, but also reds, including a delicate Pinot Noir. Thomas Shaw, the Managing Director, explains that a favourable microclimate makes it possible to produce red wines as well as the more traditional English white wines. The vineyard sits in between Malvern, the Cotswolds and the Black Mountains, in a corridor that gets half the national average rainfall – but most of it's falling today. The Severn river is relatively close and that helps keep frosts away in winter.

It seems appropriate that our visit coincides with the wettest August for 80 years because it allows us to pose the question – is this really the era of English wines?

Certainly the popularity of English wines has gone through the roof in the last couple of years, with the craze for all things organic, seasonal and local. Martin Fowke, the winemaker at Three Choirs, says their biggest problem at the moment is keeping up with demand. A growing taste for less alcoholic, less full-bodied wines has also increased interest in the English vineyards. With weather like this, less alcoholic and less full-bodied shouldn't be a problem. And some very good wine is now being made in England.

At Three Choirs they have 16 grape varieties planted over their 75 acres and they can produce up to 300,000 bottles a year.

Carbon footprint:
Wine buyers in the UK are increasingly asking themselves, why buy something made on the other side of the world when you've got something good made on your doorstep? The next couple of years could see a doubling of acreage under vine in the UK – the wine world is starting to take us very seriously.

Oz: English wine was known to be decent sometimes; it is now being recognised as good more often than not. There are several reasons for this. One is that English winemakers are experimenting with grapes that ripen more quickly and are more appropriate to the climate here. But also that climate has changed: importantly, night time temperatures are milder and daily minimum temperatures are higher, so there is less frost, and more grapes survive and ripen. Even in summers like 2008, but God knows how.

At Three Choirs the main criterion for the variety selection is that the grape must ripen quickly. But new early-ripening 'clones' of the classic Pinot Noir and Chardonnay grapes – which manage to ripen in English conditions – mean that Pinot and Chardonnay are now England's leading varieties. Unbelievable. These are the classic Burgundy grapes. And of course they are also the main grape varieties of the most famous fizz in the world: Champagne.

While Martin is planting some Pinot Noir, he isn't planting Chardonnay – he's trying to innovate rather than replicate classic Old World wines.

This is all heartening stuff. **As far as the future is concerned, Martin Fowke sees that there will be a shift from people talking about English wines to talking about Kent or South West wines** – in the same way that people don't talk about 'French' wine but about Bordeaux or Burgundy or the Loire. In Kent you get chalky soils, which make for steely wines, whereas here the soil is quite sandy, which gives a softer, more rounded fruit. These distinctions are likely to become better known and the differences emphasised.

I'm not very good at spitting – I have to drink. It's a matter of principle.

 Enough of the theory. We need to get our noses into this wine. Perched on the rain-sodden table overlooking the vines are eight wines that have been crafted from this beautiful landscape. James immediately makes a claim for the passenger seat.

The wines remind James of steam engines and traction oil on the nose, while Oz picks up cricket bat linseed oil, English hedgerows and elderflowers. We realise that our noses have discovered smells that we associate with good things, which is a big compliment to the wines produced here.

GRAPE VARIETIES FOR THE ENGLISH CLIMATE

BACCHUS
Aromatic, very English hedgerow and elderflower smell. Has low yields and therefore intense flavours.

HUXELREBE
This is commonly used in sweet wines as it is prone to botrytis – the so-called noble rot of Sauternes fame – it has good sugar levels and a distinctive rich character. It develops in the bottle to show even more character.

MADELEINE ANGEVINE
This ripens early. It is full and fruity with a fruity bouquet.

ORION
New hybrid variety. Not used as much as Phoenix.

PHOENIX
Another new hybrid – a cross between Seyval Blanc and Bacchus. No one seems to know what it tastes like.

REICHENSTEINER
This can be a little too prolific, so needs to be carefully managed. But it is an effective blending grape, without much personality of its own.

SEYVAL BLANC
A hybrid, producing high yields of good clean grapes. The wine produced is less fruity than some others, but this makes it good for blending, for aging in oak and for sparkling wine production.

SIEGERREBE
The earliest-ripening variety, commonly harvested in mid-September. Isn't prolific, so the quality is very good. It has high sugar content, low acidity and a very aromatic spicy flavour.

DORNFELDER
Lighter than Rondo and more difficult to ripen. When it is fully ripe it has a lovely purple colour and attractive plum- and damson-scented character.

PINOT NOIR
The classic Burgundy grape. New clones make it better suited to grow in England as they ripen earlier. It is used at Three Choirs to add complexity to the reds, to make a light, dryish rosé, and as a constituent of the sparkling wine.

RONDO
Very deep colour and bare-knuckle-bruiser character – new for England and will certainly make our reds darker – but don't expect subtlety.

TRIOMPHE
This ripens early, has a good fruit character and reasonable colour. Because it ripens early it has time to ripen fully, which gives it the character.

Three Choirs, Gwatkin and Tyrrells inspire us to imagine a Britain producing top-quality drinks for all palates, using the best of our national food resources. **So it's with a heavy heart that we pull over at the side of the M4 when we espy the Magor Brewery** — a giant carbuncle on the UK drinks industry's backside, according to Oz.

Oz: They produce something like eight per cent of British beer and look at it, James — there is no sense of place, no character or soul. They're not using local products like Tyrrells' potatoes, which give heart to the drink, or working with their surroundings to craft something unique and of its time and place, like Three Choirs. They're not even using British hops and barley half the time.

James: I agree that basic mass-produced lagers are absolute dogs' piss, and I really can't imagine why anybody drinks them other than to get ratted. You end up so colossally flatulent. But this is a difference between you and me — you care what other people drink, and I don't. If people want to drink lager from a megakeggery in Wales, that's all right, as long as I don't have to.

Oz: No — life should be better, life is made better with more flavour and character in your drink. And we can help. This stuff, from the barons of brewing, is industrial swill, which means that if you're daft enough to overindulge, even your hangovers are worse.

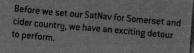

Before we set our SatNav for Somerset and cider country, we have an exciting detour to perform.

For several days now, our respective caravan brews have been bubbling away as the barley malt, yeast and water do their magic. Now it's time to go head to head at the Worcester Homebrew Challenge.

HOMEBREW CHALLENGE

OZ VERSUS JAMES

Our fun category in the Worcester Homebrew Challenge, as judged by CAMRA!

James's home brew was made using natural stolen ingredients and a German electric brewing engine. Oz's home brew was made using unacceptable 'malt extract' and some saucepans borrowed from a hotel. But Oz wins in the eyes of the CAMRA judges. So that's a victory for British pluck over the might of the Teutonic industrial machine. And bloody annoying.

7

The secret world of happy juice

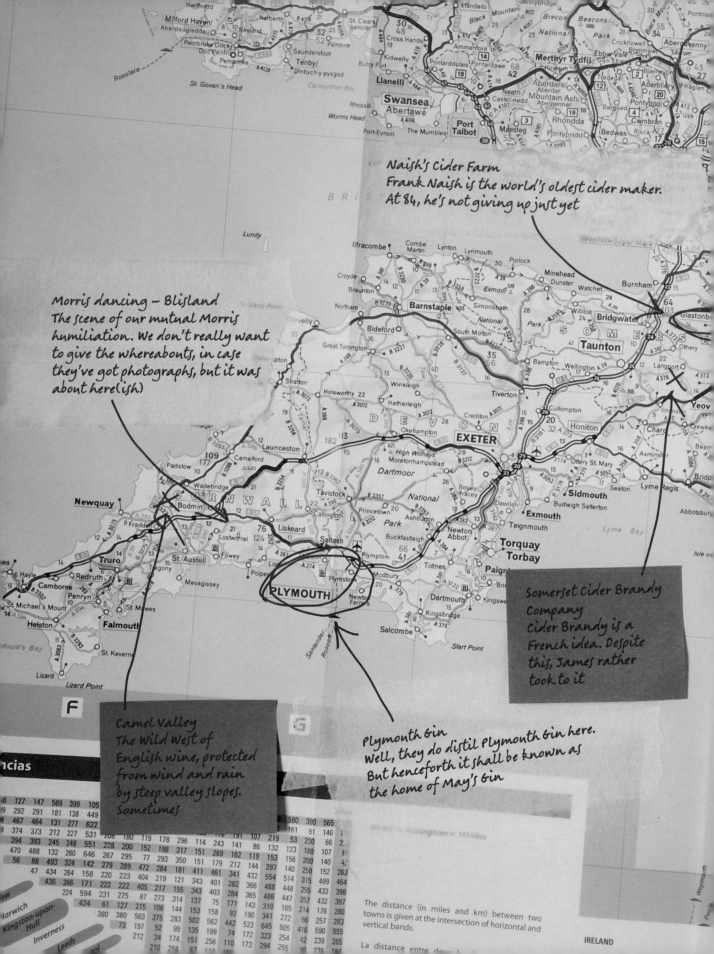

Naish's Cider Farm
Frank Naish is the world's oldest cider maker. At 84, he's not giving up just yet

Morris dancing – Blisland
The scene of our mutual Morris humiliation. We don't really want to give the whereabouts, in case they've got photographs, but it was about here(ish)

Somerset Cider Brandy Company
Cider Brandy is a French idea. Despite this, James rather took to it

Camel Valley
The Wild West of English wine, protected from wind and rain by steep valley slopes. Sometimes

Plymouth Gin
Well, they do distil Plymouth Gin here. But henceforth it shall be known as the home of May's Gin

The distance (in miles and km) between two towns is given at the intersection of horizontal and vertical bands.

La distance entre deux

CHAPTER 7:
THE SECRET WORLD
OF HAPPY JUICE

Cider has a good claim to be the drink of England
– if not of Britain. It has been made here for a long, long time and
at certain points in our island's history looked as if it might become
our national brew. But cider's story since ale became dominant in the
late 17th century has been one of survival. It has been the subject
of repeated revival attempts and is currently in the midst of one of
these. We have come to Somerset to talk to two exponents of the art
of making apples into happy juice – could it be that we are going to
reclaim cider as the proper drink of Britain?

Oz's firkin of

CIDER HISTORY

The Celts and the Romans certainly knew something about the potential for apples to make a satisfying pint, but it was the Normans who gave cider the first real push to become the brew of choice in the British Isles. The preference for ale and cider see-sawed for much of the Middle Ages. **Then early in the 17th century the Puritans decided to throw their religious might behind planting apple trees and, by implication, cider**. When farmers planted apple trees they often had too many apples to sell, so they preserved their excess crop by making it into cider, and this started a ball rolling. It also meant that we didn't have to rely on imported wine to get sozzled – we could brew our own means of inebriation without any outside interference. Given how often England was at war with virtually everybody until the 19th century, cider had a lot going for it.

Cider was thought to match wine for subtlety of flavour. Advances in technology helped produce more and more sophisticated, safe and interesting brews. As cider techniques got better and better, so its popularity grew. It was in danger of becoming a serious challenge to foreign wine imports, with vintages being declared and the really good stuff reserved for the wealthy.

Cider drinking was such second nature in country areas that farm workers were given a daily allowance of two quarts (one quart for boys). Well, a lot more during August and throughout the harvest, but they had better summers then and haymaking is thirsty work!

128

But at the point at which people started to consider cider seriously as being our national drink, the money men appeared. When the 18th-century equivalents of today's big brewers (cider merchants and middle men) noticed cider's success, they saw an opportunity to make a lot of money. **As soon as this large-scale profit motive appeared, the emphasis was placed on quantity and the quality of the cider slumped.** Apple pulp was watered down (the apples were twice milled, with water added to the second milling). The cider merchants started to produce a drink that they thought more suited the public taste – i.e. made in a way more profitable for them. Like the megakeggery approach to beer production, cidermaking was reduced to the lowest common denominator; flavour and individuality were stifled. This, coupled with changes to tax law that made cider as expensive to produce as it was to import foreign wine, meant that cider was fighting a losing battle. It became less attractive to make and this coincided with the rise of the big brewing houses – Whitbread and Bass and the like – in the late 18th century.

CIDER AS MEDICINE

Cider was also meant to be medicinal; according to folklore it was responsible for curing or seeing off:

scurvy
gallstones
disease of the spleen
melancholy
dropsy
the ague
the lumpy
the oozy
trench foot
spots

before cider   after cider

There's probably some medical truth to this

It was also widely held to be excellent against rheumatism, as this old verse testifies:

'Wold Zam could never goe vur long
Wi'out his jar of virkin
A used the Zider zame's twur ile
To keep his jints vrim quirken'

Which James translates as: Old Sam could never go for long
Without a pull from his small barrel
And he used cider in the same way as I did
To keep his joints from making a creaking noise

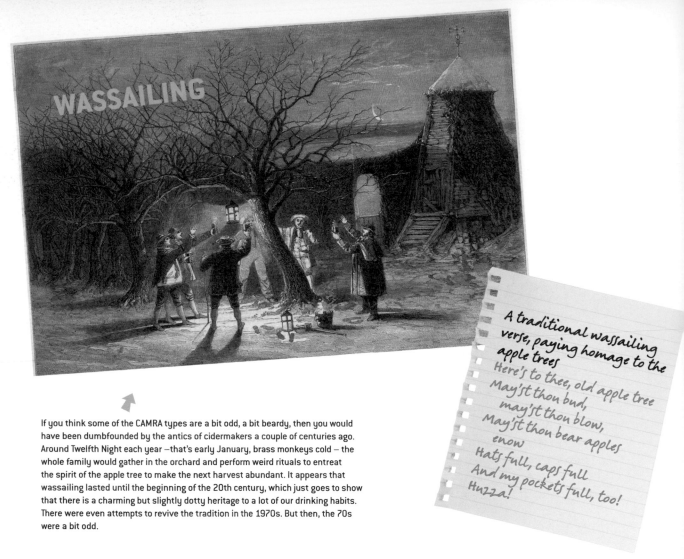

WASSAILING

If you think some of the CAMRA types are a bit odd, a bit beardy, then you would have been dumbfounded by the antics of cidermakers a couple of centuries ago. Around Twelfth Night each year —that's early January, brass monkeys cold — the whole family would gather in the orchard and perform weird rituals to entreat the spirit of the apple tree to make the next harvest abundant. It appears that wassailing lasted until the beginning of the 20th century, which just goes to show that there is a charming but slightly dotty heritage to a lot of our drinking habits. There were even attempts to revive the tradition in the 1970s. But then, the 70s were a bit odd.

A traditional wassailing verse, paying homage to the apple trees

Here's to thee, old apple tree
May'st thou bud,
may'st thou blow,
May'st thou bear apples
enow
Hats full, caps full
And my pockets full, too!
Huzza!

Over years and generations, cider has attempted many times to reinstate itself on our national consciousness. James feels that it made rather too heavy an impression in his youth and as a result he feels queasy even at the sight of a 3-litre brown plastic bottle of the stuff. I try to tell him he was drinking the cider equivalent of Welsh-brewed 'premium lager'. Even so, we approach our first stop with some reluctance.

THE OLDEST CIDER MAKER
IN THE WORLD *probably*

Frank Naish

Frank Naish is 84. He has been making cider since he was about five, although his memory is a little hazy on that point. He is probably the oldest cider maker in Britain, if not the world – although he can't remember. If ever there was an honest yeoman of England, he is it. The house he has lived in nearly all his life has remained pretty much untouched since the day his grandparents moved in in 1919. He only got electricity in 2003 – apparently because candles were getting too expensive. He sells his cider to callers at his farm and wholesalers. He has absolutely no idea where the wholesalers sell his cider, but thinks it might be at local fairs. What he enjoys and has done for the past 80-odd years is making the stuff. He is ably assisted by Paul Chant, who joined him a few years ago and has that infectious enthusiasm of someone who has found what they love in life. He gives us the sprint version of cidermaking:

Paul: Mill the apples, which means bash them around until they're a bit pulverised; shovel the pomace (which is the bruised apples) out and build a cheese.

James: A what?

Paul: A cheese. To do that we start off with a square – a wooden frame about 2 foot square. Then we put a cider cloth in there; then we put the pomace in and wrap it up. Then we lift it up, put some wood in between and do the same again. That's a cake. There's ten cakes to make a cheese. Then we press it down and all the juice comes out. We take the juice to the barrel and it starts to ferment. The leftover pulp we give to the pigs. There are no additives. No chemicals in any of the process. It's just fermented apple juice and it's bloody good stuff.

Paul explains the nuts and bolts of cidermaking.

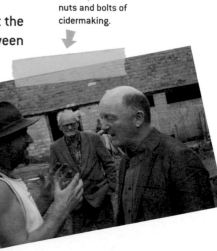

Oz: How do you decide which apples to use?

Paul: We just experiment 'til we get something we like. Between 20 and 30 different apple types can go into any one pressing. You could use just one sort but it's much better to take a mixture 'cos you get more interesting flavours. There are basically four types of apple (bittersharps, sharps, bittersweets and sweets) and the combination of these types is what makes interesting cider. Oh, but don't use the Ten Commandments – they're rubbish!

Oz: So do you aim for a consistent taste?

Paul: No, not really – each cask is distinctive. That's the beauty of it. Years ago they used to distil some of it too, to make cider brandy – they say it tasted like paint stripper, but gorgeous paint stripper.

James gingerly lifts a glass, sips and ... smiles. This is good stuff. He sips again and then takes a long swig. Oz is still sniffing. The 'Who's driving?' discussion is resolved without a word spoken. James is on his second pint by the time Oz notices. Can this be the James May who has been unable even to hear the word cider throughout his adult life without developing St Vitus's dance? Paul goes on to say that he likes to categorise his cider into easy-drinking, fighting, singing and sleeping. Before the Government leap on their responsible drinking hobby horse, the kind of fighting he's talking about is the sort where you get 100,000 well-oiled Englishmen on a field facing their enemy with muskets and swords: Civil War – which Paul thinks happens every year when 'the hippies come to Pilton'.

James is on to the singing style before Oz has managed to spit out the easy-drinking cider. It's very good stuff. James is reciting poetry in

a broad Somerset accent. 'What's he on about?' asks Frank. 'Search me,' says Paul, 'can't understand a word'. A demon has been banished from James's life, though his Ziderzet accent will haunt Frank for many a long night.

The classic food to eat with cider is of course cheese. We're presented with a huge block of locally produced Cheddar and the combination is mouth-watering – the brilliant cheese steals away the bitterness of the cider and replaces it with a sublime mellow softness. It makes perfect sense that two locally produced products should work in such harmony. 'But whose Cheddar is it?' Oz demands, 'Oh, it's from my cousin over Shepton way. I give her five gallons of cider, she gives me a truckle.' Paul cuts the cheese with a sword from the Monmouth rebellion in 1688. James is still reciting doggerel.

We roll out of Naish's Cider Farm convinced that cider deserves a central place in Britain's drinking culture. And we're not talking megakeggery alcoholic apple juice here – we're talking real cider made from the juice of actual cider apples. By guys like Frank and Paul.

After a few glasses, James unleashes his vocal chords with songs and poetry. Frank is clearly moved.

Burrow Hill Cider & THE SOMERSET DISTILLERY.

OF APPLES AND BRANDY

The copper stills at
Burrow Hill Farm

If Frank Naish epitomises the survival part of the cidermaking story, our next encounter is with someone who is trying to use the tradition to revive a lost part of the 'apple into delicious alcoholic drink' story. He is Julian Temperley and he cares about apples and cider. Really cares. He owns The Somerset Cider Brandy Company in the heart of Somerset and believes that good cider can easily stand up to good wine in the taste stakes. We've come to taste something rather stronger than that, though. **The production of cider brandy in Britain dates back to the late 17th century** and it is for this beautiful drink that we have turned up.

Inevitably there is a comparison to be made with Calvados, the French apple brandy, but as we're English and we're on a British adventure we ignore it. **What's the point of importing stuff from the French when we make this delicious British spirit here?** All sorts of appley-delicious notes fill Oz's mouth as we try the range of brandies from three to 20 years old.

The impressive thing about the set-up is that it uses the best local produce to make a really first-rate local drink, steeped in the traditions of the region. But more than that, what Julian is doing is taking the best ideas from the world of winemaking and applying those that are appropriate to his cider brandy and vintage cidermaking. There is a real sense of revival here and it gives us heart after the depressing sight of Wales's megakeggery.

Off to Cornwall. Have we got our passports?

Oz and James find shelter from the sun in Julian Temperley's apple orchard before sharing a glass of cider with the dog.

A day or two on the ground as windfalls doesn't do cider apples any harm and reduces the need to employ children to climb the trees.

THE CORNISH PASTY

Terroir is a French term, used to denote the special characteristics that geography bestows upon wine. It roughly means 'a sense of place' reflected in the wine's qualities, and in the unique contribution that local environment makes – how the soil the vines are grown in affects flavour, for instance.

Can there be a terroir of Cornish pasties? The Cornish Pasty Association certainly thinks so, and is submitting an application to the European Commission for the pasty to be granted Protected Geographical Indication (PGI) status, which currently applies to products like Parma ham and Champagne. This would mean that only traditional pasty makers in Cornwall would be able to use the label 'Cornish pasty'.

Traditionalists maintain that **a genuine Cornish pasty has a distinctive 'D' shape and is crimped on one side, never on top.** The texture of the filling for the pasty must be chunky, made up of uncooked beef, swede or turnip, potato and onion and a light peppery seasoning. It must be made in Cornwall, of course.

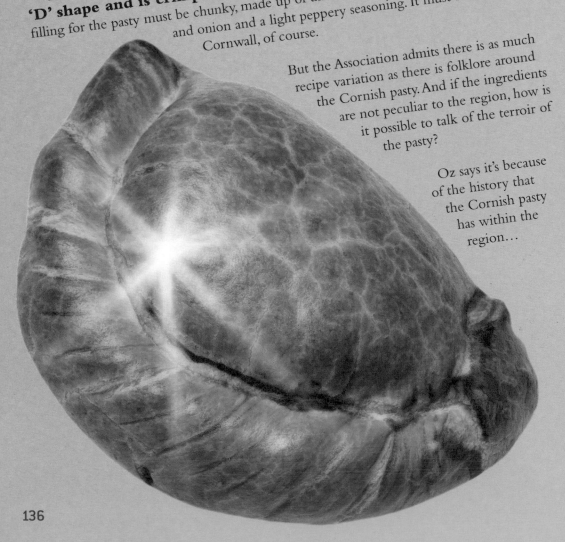

But the Association admits there is as much recipe variation as there is folklore around the Cornish pasty. And if the ingredients are not peculiar to the region, how is it possible to talk of the terroir of the pasty?

Oz says it's because of the history that the Cornish pasty has within the region…

James will do anything to avoid Morris dancing – including wearing a silly hat, a silly shirt, and taking up the recorder. Meanwhile Oz fights his way out of a lock-in at the local through a horde of retired bank managers.

Oz and Sam Lindo discuss the quintessential terroir of English wine amid the quintessential terroir of an English caravan.

CAMEL VALLEY – A VERY ENGLISH VINEYARD

Another uplifting sight greets us as we steer the bouncing caravan – by now with its unique terroir – towards a famous English vineyard. Camel Valley nestles in a valley with an extraordinarily favourable aspect. The slope is very steep, so that the sun hits it at a good angle for grape production, and there is a bend at the end of the valley that wards off the rain and softens the westerly Cornish winds blowing through the vineyard. Except today, of course. Pissing down. But Bob and Sam Lindo swear it is an ideal spot with an ideal microclimate to produce excellent wine; they've been making English wine here since 1986 – to great international acclaim. They are keen to stress the Englishness of what they are doing. Bob's intention (he is the father of the father-son combination) is to reproduce the flavours and characteristics of English fruit in the wine rather than try to replicate French wines, which most of the world seems to want to do. He is, in other words, trying to establish an English style.

So the Bacchus he produces is light, fresh, with medium alcohol, and has the quintessentially English smell of elderflower. His fizz has a hint of strawberry – English strawberry – and very ripe Bramley apples. The point is that it smells and tastes of fruit that is English – it doesn't come from anywhere else.

James notices the English equivalent of the AC system emblazoned on the bottle. It is PSR – Product of a Specified Region, and that region is England. That's it? Just England? Yup. As specific as that.

James's wine notes

1. Bacchus might be, at the moment, the definitive white wine of England.

2. Fish and chips go perfectly with English wines.

strawberry

elderflower

fish and chips

Camel Valley sparkling wine has won numerous awards; most recently it was judged to be one of the world's top fizzes, second only to a Bollinger Champagne.

138

THAT JEKYLL AND HYDE SPIRIT

Our next encounter is with a drink that we have adopted and made our own. If our next drink makes you think of anything, it is of refreshment on an English summer's evening. **It is the tipple of middle England**. It is, of course, gin. And gin, like cider, has had something of a revival in the past 20 years.

Gin has a lot of historical associations for us Brits. From the rancid Gin Lane of Hogarth's time to the Gin and It of the English middle classes, it seems to have been all things to all Britons at various stages in its history. We have to consider it as a contender for the drink that defines Britain, if only for the fact that every class and section of society has got hammered on it in one way or another for more than 400 years.

Gin was first produced in Holland as a medicine, and flavoured with juniper to make it more palatable. Supposedly it cured leprosy and 'cholic', which in those days meant virtually any illness that wasn't leprosy or bilharzia. In the early 17th century, English troops developed a taste for 'Dutch courage' while fighting in the Thirty Years' War, when they saw how the Dutch swigged back gallons of the stuff before battle and then fought with devil-may-care bravery. Luckily, the English were on the same side, and they took the taste for gin home with them.

When William of Orange came to the English throne in 1689, he made it possible for anyone to distil spirits; previously the right to distil had been guarded jealously. The quality was often very poor, but it was cheap, even compared with beer, and consumption grew wildly. By 1730, there were more than 7,000 shops selling spirits in London alone.

Gin was blamed for mass drunkenness – hey, drunkenness? – death and destitution, too. 'Drunk for a penny, dead drunk for twopence' wasn't just a harmless ditty in the 1700s. London's population was shrinking because everyone was too clattered to do what comes naturally, even to the semi-sober. Today's binge drinkers are Sunday school teachers by comparison. The artist William Hogarth depicted the worst effects in his engravings of 1751, which contrasted the evils of 'Gin Lane' (right) with the productive, happy patriotism of 'Beer Street' (far right).

139

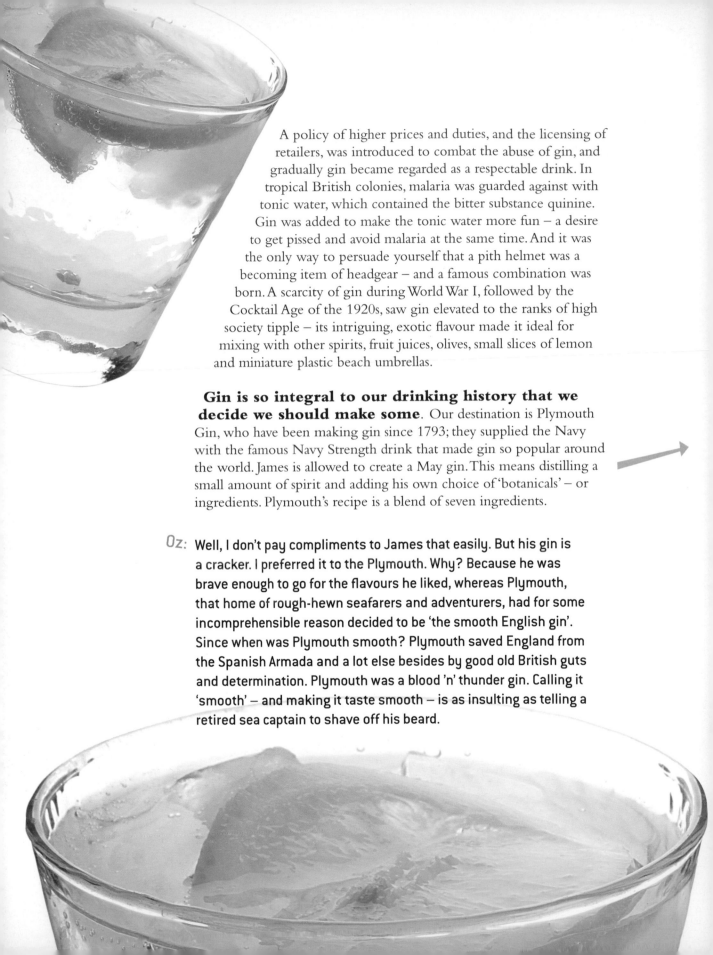

A policy of higher prices and duties, and the licensing of retailers, was introduced to combat the abuse of gin, and gradually gin became regarded as a respectable drink. In tropical British colonies, malaria was guarded against with tonic water, which contained the bitter substance quinine. Gin was added to make the tonic water more fun – a desire to get pissed and avoid malaria at the same time. And it was the only way to persuade yourself that a pith helmet was a becoming item of headgear – and a famous combination was born. A scarcity of gin during World War I, followed by the Cocktail Age of the 1920s, saw gin elevated to the ranks of high society tipple – its intriguing, exotic flavour made it ideal for mixing with other spirits, fruit juices, olives, small slices of lemon and miniature plastic beach umbrellas.

Gin is so integral to our drinking history that we decide we should make some. Our destination is Plymouth Gin, who have been making gin since 1793; they supplied the Navy with the famous Navy Strength drink that made gin so popular around the world. James is allowed to create a May gin. This means distilling a small amount of spirit and adding his own choice of 'botanicals' – or ingredients. Plymouth's recipe is a blend of seven ingredients.

Oz: Well, I don't pay compliments to James that easily. But his gin is a cracker. I preferred it to the Plymouth. Why? Because he was brave enough to go for the flavours he liked, whereas Plymouth, that home of rough-hewn seafarers and adventurers, had for some incomprehensible reason decided to be 'the smooth English gin'. Since when was Plymouth smooth? Plymouth saved England from the Spanish Armada and a lot else besides by good old British guts and determination. Plymouth was a blood 'n' thunder gin. Calling it 'smooth' – and making it taste smooth – is as insulting as telling a retired sea captain to shave off his beard.

JAMES'S BOTANICALS MIX

Plymouth use seven ingredients (sorry 'botanicals') to flavour their gin, but I went for a more modest six. However, I also added a twist of something a little spicy, for a rather satisfying drink.

Cardamom pods (crushed so the taste of the seed is prevalent). This is the spicy twist

Angelina Jolie (well, angelica root actually, but it annoys O2 if I use the wrong name)

Orris root (which helps to bind the other flavours together)

Lemon peel

Juniper (all gins are based on juniper). Genièvre is the French word for juniper. Genever became the Dutch word for juniper-flavoured gin, and we just called it 'gin'.

Coriander seeds

The botanicals are boiled over a bunsen burner.

The result of the experiment is excellent – a drink that we agree would go well with a curry.

An interlude on

THE JOYS OF CARAVAN LIVING

Plan of Sprite 78, days 1–8

Sartorial storage area (wardrobe):
OC – pink dressing gown + bathers (unused)
JM – crash helmet + pen knife

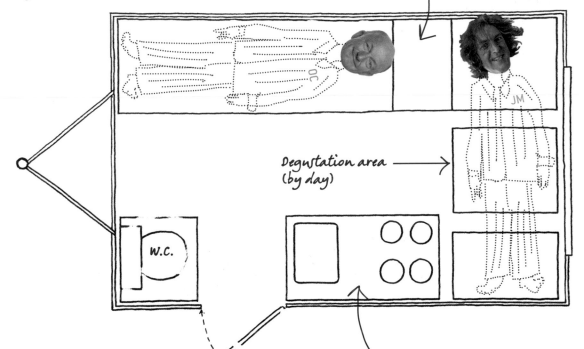

Degustation area (by day)

caravan portal – gateway to the world

Cooking and cleaning zone, containing all the culinary essentials for happy caravan living – tea bags, spam, beans, salad cream, tomato sauce, cheese

W.C.

broken

To make room for James's copper behemoth, Oz had to settle for an ad hoc sleeping arrangement in the former degustation area, while James found the floor the most reliable place to bed down.

JM Brewery (the German kit)

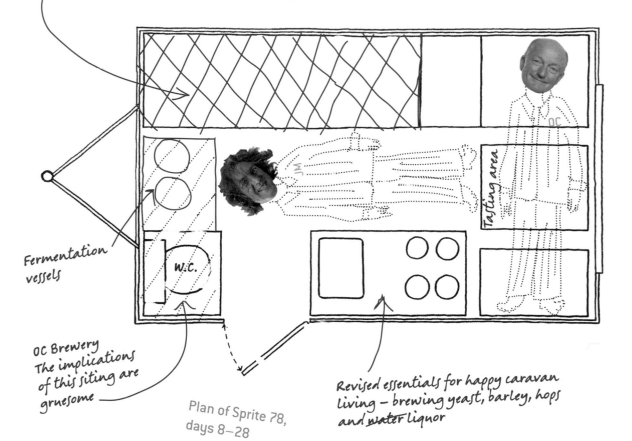

Fermentation vessels

OC Brewery
The implications of this siting are gruesome

Plan of Sprite 78, days 8–28

Revised essentials for happy caravan living — brewing yeast, barley, hops and ~~water~~ liquor

THE SPRITE LIFE

A new day dawns in the caravan and Oz is reborn as a new man, free of care and worry. And that's before he's eaten the spam'n'beans.

Having been on the road for about four weeks now, it is time to reflect on the benefits and drawbacks of life on the open road with a Sprite 78 (or, for compliance reasons, any other caravan).

James: The window sills are rotten, the skylight has a big hole in it (very useful for English summers), the bottle containing the dangerous toilet chemicals leaked over our unused brand new towels, the door flies open as you're driving (slowly) up the motorway and the curtains don't close in the middle — apart from that it's the height of luxury.

Oz: And the bed makes you tense. If you decide to turn over, you have to steel yourself because a few seconds of solitary activity (and I do only mean turning over) invariably leads to the collapse of the bed. It says something for what passed as luxury holidaying in 1978 that, at best, you would only fall out of bed three times in the night.

James: And the cooking — I realised in the complex preparation of spam and beans that we needed a chopping board. One of the sprites (did I really say that?) went to the shops and came back with a set of three. But anything more than what you absolutely need in the caravan is something you can't afford. We had to throw two out because otherwise there simply isn't space to work. The 1970s were about what you needed to get by rather than what you wanted.

144

Braver men than Oz have recoiled at the odour of a freshly boiled haggis. Protected by his pink dressing gown-cum-pinny and with James offering encouragement from the rear, Oz bares his nostrils to the sonsie-faced one.

Oz: And you need to be careful which signature dish you choose.

James: Yes. Ours is very much spam and beans, but in a caravan you need to make sure that whatever you cook requires the minimum of bodily movement.

Some words you could use for caravan life: shit, rubbish, small, cramped, damp, smelly, irritating. Oz Clarke.

On that positive note, we move on to our next area of exploration. On the way we have time to consider the claims of cider, cider brandy and gin to be the drink that defines Britain. Cider clearly has the strongest claim: a long history, and made from ingredients that occur in abundance here without the need to import anything (apart from a bit of know-how). It certainly is a contender. Gin didn't originate in these Isles in the same way that whisky did, so it has less of a claim, although it can be seen to represent the essence of Englishness in the classic G&T. Cider brandy is still too obscure, we feel, to have more than a whisper of a claim.

We're heading back to where we started. It gives us an opportunity to reflect on what we've learnt along the way and **to decide which drink best represents Britain today**.

8

Dreamers
and
dreams

Scotney Castle
This bit of Kent was once the world's most important hop region. Now it's just Ian Strang and a couple of mates

Westerham Brewery
Westerham brewed the beer that fuelled the Battle of Britain pilots. Despite which, they shot down an awful lot of Messerschmitts

'Never in the field of human conflict was so much owed by so many to so few'

Winston Churchill,
August 1940

White Cliffs of Dover, where our adventure began and ended

Oz born here!

Tunnel-sous la Manche
Channel Tunnel

Breaky Bottom
Home to Peter Hall,
English wine's original dreamer of dreamers

THE FRENCH!!!
They come over here, they buy up our vineyard land ...

Wiston Estate
Possible site of England's greatest vineyard. It's not planted yet

CHAPTER 8: DREAMERS AND DREAMS

So we head back towards Dover and reflect on what we've discovered on this grand tour of the British Isles. One aspect of the British booze 'industry' that we have seen rather too much of is the marketing-led, lowest-common-denominator, passionless mass production of drink. But while we agree that the taste is, well, tasteless, we disagree about what we think about the mass production aspect of it. James feels that if people want to drink it, that's fine; there's no harm in it and if people decide that they want something else, they can go and get it. **Oz, who James suspects has Communist tendencies, wants people to be able to drink better drinks** – he cares that the beer of mass production is shoddy, tasteless and full of chemicals. It's a fundamental disagreement we can't resolve.

It's also a useful backdrop to our final few visits, because our intention is to meet some passionate producers of wine and beer. People who care about taste, how things are made and what they produce. They're dreamers, but **dreamers with a steely determination to get their lovingly crafted drinks to a wide audience**.

Our first stop is to meet a man who doesn't just have a daydream, he has a full-scale, seven-days-and-nights epic of a dream. Dermot Sugrue has already got 16 acres of prime Sussex chalk downland planted with the classic Champagne grape varieties: Chardonnay, Pinot Noir and Pinot Meunier. But he wants more. His dream is, eventually, to produce the best grand cru 'Champagne' in the world and he's identified a gorgeous south-facing horseshoe-shaped crescent of downland chalk that soaks up the sun and is protected from the wind. **'England's Grand F****** Cru', he cries**. And I have to say, it looks like a classic vineyard site to me. Except for one thing. It doesn't have any vines. Yet. Of course, owing to EC guidelines, Dermot can't call it Champagne because the French have trademarked that, but he can make wine in the traditional Champagne method.

Dermot's looking for investment. He offers James a slice for 50 grand. And James is tempted. Wow! The guy who thinks fizz is just for men in tights and chorus girls is thinking of taking a slice of English sparkling action.

Dermot Sugrue (at the wheel)

Oh God, off we go again, up to look at Dermot's imaginary field of grapes.

But, hold on a second, **who says the French invented Champagne?** There is a very good claim that one Christopher Merrett 'discovered' the Champagne method in London in 1662, well before Messrs Bollinger, Pérignon or Madame Clicquot got their knickers in a twizzle stick.

THE TERROIR!!! again!

WHO 'INVENTED' CHAMPAGNE ANYWAY?

Until the 18th century, Champagne was a still wine. Records show that the first mention in France of sparkling wine was in 1718 and in that document it notes that the drink first appeared in about 1695. However, in England, 30–plus years *before* that, sparkling Champagne was certainly available in England and, perhaps even more surprising, was already incredibly popular.

Tom Stevenson, in his *World Encyclopedia of Champagne and Sparkling Wine*, quotes a verse from George Etherege's 1676 work 'The Man of Mode':

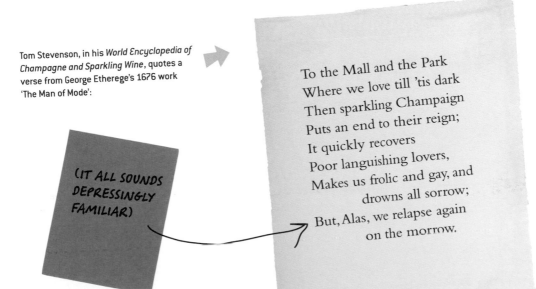

To the Mall and the Park
Where we love till 'tis dark
Then sparkling Champaign
Puts an end to their reign;
It quickly recovers
Poor languishing lovers,
Makes us frolic and gay, and
drowns all sorrow;
But, Alas, we relapse again
on the morrow.

(IT ALL SOUNDS DEPRESSINGLY FAMILIAR)

151

So how is that England was producing Champagne before, well, the wine producers in Champagne? There appear to be a few technical factors as well as one key scientific one. England managed to produce much stronger glass earlier than the French – so the bottles could withstand the pressure exerted by the fizzy wine; also, the cork technology lost after the Romans left both England and France was rediscovered much earlier in England than in France. The result was that England 'had the technology' decades before France did.

But who 'invented' the Champagne method? It seems clear that **fizzing, effervescent wine had been accidentally made for centuries** (it is even mentioned in the Bible), but there is documentary evidence – in a paper presented by Christopher Merrett to the Royal Society in 1662 – that the English had been deliberately making fizzy wine 30 years before the French made their first sparkling Champagne. Merrett's paper says:

'our wine-coopers of recent times use vast quantities of sugar and molasses to all sorts of wines to make them drink brisk and sparkling'.

In fact it seems that the man whom the French worship as the patron saint of Champagne, Dom Pérignon, spent a good deal of his life trying to get rid of the bubbles from his wine rather than keeping them in it.

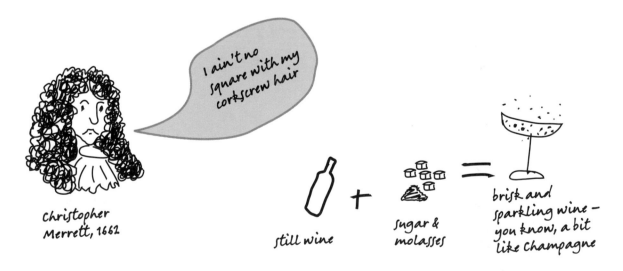

I ain't no square with my corkscrew hair

christopher Merrett, 1662

still wine + sugar & molasses = brisk and sparkling wine – you know, a bit like champagne

Dermot has invested in a traditional Champagne press – a Coquard press. These machines are the gentle presses that are crucially important for the serious Champagne producers in France – they have a huge surface area, which means that the pressing is very light and the juice extracted is delicate and – in the case of the black Pinot Noir grapes – colourless. Rougher wooden presses would produce pink juice, or even red.

In an astonishing turnaround in technology views, though, James is disappointed in this new machine, while Oz can barely contain his excitement. James feels this mechanical behemoth lacks 'terroir' and is somehow inauthentic. Oz is trembling at the thought that **traditional Champagne methods and equipment** are going to be used to hoist Britain to Champagne's heights as a fizz producer. It's a bizarre moment for us as we accuse each other of treachery to our own causes. Sadly, though, we can't put the machine to the test; the first wine from the Wiston Estate won't be ready for another ten years or so. **We decide that we have to taste some English sparkling wine to assess the future**. There's another problem though. James is still not sure that he likes sparkling wine – or indeed sparkling anything.

James: I've decided that sparkling is a word I don't like – it's spineless and limp. Sparkling water, sparkling people, sparkling entertainment, sparkling evening, sparkling shoes, sparkling sequin tops on TV presenters: it's not a word that is applied to anything I like. Sparkling wit means 'boring' and someone who has it is best avoided at parties. And this applies to wine because of the bubbles – they are transient, they burst forth and come to naught. They're an allegory for a shallow life.

Oz: God, you're a miserable old sod sometimes. Why don't you think of bubbles as brief spurts of pleasure which fade away from you and then you're ready for the next one. They aren't supposed to be permanent; their impermanence is their joy. Their ability to give you a temporary lift, a temporary transportation to a higher plane of joy is their *raison d'être*. We have to enjoy bubbles for what they are.

The worst drink ever to sully these shores is mineral water. Mineral water, whether 'refreshingly sparkling' or 'delightfully still', is an affront to the civil engineers who gave us a fresh water supply from the tap.
They did not spend centuries perfecting a system of nationwide plumbing so that some ponce in France could bottle his local bilharzia-ridden stream and ship it over to us in designer bottles.

BREAKY BOTTOM

Peter Hall makes English fizz – and still wine, and liqueur –
in one of the most beautiful spots in England. He has been
making wine at Breaky Bottom, nestled in stunning Sussex
countryside, since 1974. It has been a struggle and it always
will be, but the point about Peter and what he does at Breaky
Bottom is that he has no plans to expand – despite repeated
critical acclaim – he just wants to carry on improving and
making excellent wine. The dream is one step on from
Dermot's. Peter is now living it. Peter Hall simply wants
to make the best wine that he can from his little corner of
paradise in the South Downs.

Peter Hall is a thoughtful winemaker.
What's he thinking about? Will he
get a crop this year? Will the frosts
or pests get his grapes? Or will they
ripen triumphantly in the deep chalk
folds of the Downs? And the wine he
makes – how much pleasure will it
give? And will James May drink all
of it?

155

JAMES'S BLIND TASTING NOTES

Deep in the Sussex countryside, Peter Hall and Oz try to cure James of his aversion to fizz in the same way that we conquered his cider-phobia – by letting him drink lots of it – this time in the guise of a 'blind' sparkling wine tasting. There are many styles of sparkling wine – they don't all have to be Champagne. In fact James's favourite is a Californian sparkler – albeit made by one of the most famous Champagne producers.

Good acidity, good fruit, good bready quality. Some custard perhaps? **(Quartet, Roederer, California)**

Metallic nose, with a hint of body odour. But this is the light perspiration of someone you quite like, not the rancid onions of BO. There's a slight smell of old rubber from old tent fixings. It's honeyed, a bit like a breakfast cereal – can't say which one but there's honey and a monster involved.

(Tesco Finest Premier Cru Champagne, France)

Small bubbles, colour almost salmon pink, and there is a slightly fishy note on the nose. Good fishy though. It has smooth and not much acidity.

(Bloomsbury, Ridgeview, England)

The smell of the sweat of an athlete. Could probably do with five years in Oz's secret basement.

Do you know what this makes me think of? You sit down in the television room of a country hotel to watch the football or something and the hotel cat comes along and decides it wants to sit on your knee. It jumps up and circles around a few times to make a little bed for itself before it settles down. At the point before it settles you're thinking 'A cat is a nice thing, it's soft and comforting and therapeutic.' But it still hasn't settled yet, it's still thinking about which way it wants to lie. That's what this wine reminds me of.

(Breaky Bottom, England)

Not so much on the nose, more feral, almost beer-like aroma. Has an elegant if slightly overpowering sourness. **(Chapel Down, England) JOINT FIFTH**

Nose is of a well-used gearbox, burnt rubber, faintly toxic. Light fruity taste, a dry spice like cumin or fenugreek. Strange finish, slightly peppery.

(Moet & Chandon Champagne, France) JOINT FIFTH

Not much breadiness, quite acidic, good fruit, hint of citrus. **(Jansz, Tasmania)**

Medium bubbles, Amber, not salmon pink or yellow colour. Looks mature. Nose is of a skin of a peach. It's quite round – you could almost describe it as a flippant wine. Slightly blowsy.

(Nyetimber Classic Cuvée, England)

Deep yellow colour but smells of old Bibles in a damp vestry! It's corked … Oh dear. **(Codorníu cava, Spain)**

(Oz: I'm used to this. When James starts to ramble like this it means he has not been spitting – well, he refuses to learn, citing affronts to Bacchus and God knows what – so he is well on to his fifth or sixth glass by this stage…)

WESTERHAM BREWERY

An Oz by any other name ... various names of Oz Clarke as told to James May:

Oz
Robert Owen Clarke
Robbie O'Clarke of Graiguenamanagh
Owen, boyo, from the Valleys
Lord Osbert Clarke of Harrow
T'Oz Clarke from Yorkshire
Oz Clarke off the telly

Arriving back in Kent – 'home' as Oz calls it in another claim to be from yet another part of these British Isles – we meet Robert Wicks. Robert is passionate about all aspects of his brewing – its heritage, the fact that the ingredients are locally sourced and that it is putting money back into local businesses to help them to continue to supply raw materials.

Robert Wicks is an innovative revivalist brewer. Phew. What that actually means is that he is using modern methods to recreate the taste of one of the great Kent breweries.

Westerham's BB (British Bulldog) ale celebrates the nation's Battle of Britain pilots.

One of the key parts of the process, and a part that has been absolutely fundamental to the identity of Kent over the centuries, is the growing of hops. In the past 50 years, though, hops have largely disappeared from the Kent countryside and are only now showing the tiniest shoots of recovery. In a county that once set the world price for hops, this is a depressing state of affairs.

Robert takes us to one of his suppliers, Ian Strang, a hop farmer based at Scotney Castle in Lamberhurst. Ian plants hops out of a sense of tradition – it's what farmers in Kent used to do, and his Dad did it before him. He has to make

'BEER'S FINEST HOUR'

Westerham Brewery Company was established in 2004 to bring back the glory days of the old **Black Eagle Brewery**, which closed in 1965 following the consolidation of the 'big breweries' in the 1950s and 60s. So much for the revival part; the innovation comes from the fact that Robert recognised that the yeast the brewer uses imparts a substantial amount of the beer's flavour. In fact, Robert reckons, the water and the yeast can account for as much as 75 per cent of what the drinker finally tastes. So he applied to the National Collection of Yeast Cultures in Norwich (The Public Yeast Office as James christens it) to obtain a sample of the yeast used by Black Eagle before it closed down. The man responsible for depositing the yeast in 1965 was one Bill Wickett, who coincidentally was also asked to set up a brewery in North Africa during World War II when things weren't going right for our boys. He could be described as the '**man who biffed Rommel**'.

But this is not the only claim to national salvation that the Black Eagle Brewery can make – **Winston Churchill** lived round the corner in Chartwell and was known to order the **beer by the firkin**. And yet more patriotically, the fighter pilots stationed at Biggin Hill used to drink Black Eagle brews in the pubs between missions. Black Eagle was the brewery that biffed Rommel, defeated the Luftwaffe and sustained Churchill. It was perhaps beer's 'finest hour'.

No wonder that it is worth reviving.

The yeast that Robert Wicks is using may well have been used for over 200 years!

and more on yeast...

Yeast is an uncontrolled organism that frolics when it meets sugar. It turns the sugar in malted barley to alcohol, and one of the great problems in brewing has been to keep the yeast infection-free. If it gets infected it is almost impossible to clear it up and breweries have been known to close down as a result. So if you work in a brewery you have to have powdered milk in your tea because the danger of infecting the yeast from any milk that is going off is too great. **James is horrified: 'so the two great British drinks can't live together in harmony.'** Yeast is essential to the taste of the beer and its health is essential to the survival of the brewery. As each yeast will bring a different flavour, when a brewery finds one that works with its style of beer, it holds on to it for good.

Ian strang, in his hop garden

a living from other farming but he keeps going with hops because he feels it is his duty. Once, over 72,000 acres of England were planted with hops. Now there are just under 3000 acres, although this is very slowly increasing.

Against this background, Ian's decision has the bravery and commitment we have seen from both Peter and Dermot – someone who believes that what he's doing is something he just has to do. There's a wonderful quiet nobility about him. Financial common sense doesn't govern his decision to grow hops; his heart does. We gaze out at his hop garden from an oast house (these are the tepee-shaped buildings with wind cowls on top that pepper the Kent countryside and were

For those of you who don't know Kent, these are oast houses, used for drying hops. Kent has hundreds of them, though just a handful still thrill to the marvellous aroma of fresh hops each September. But why didn't the photographer wait until the shit-spreader had passed by?

OZ's HOP FACT!

"A hop field is called a 'hop garden' in Kent and a 'hop yard' in Worcestershire. In both cases, this was to avoid paying tax. By not calling it a farm or field, less duty was payable."

used for drying hops). The landscape would once have been hops as far as the eye could see.

Ian's commitment is in stark contrast to one lesson we have learnt as our tour has unfolded. The big multinational producers often extol the virtues of balance and consistency, but more often than not, balance and consistency equate to banality and rubbish. They are great 'get-out' words — what these producers make lacks anything approaching passion, ingenuity or taste. When you come to places where people believe in what they do and are prepared to take risks, then you encounter flavour and excitement.

OZ'S RANT: The huge conglomerates cut away the rough edges and the interesting bits and end up with something that's virtually the same as everyone else's or slightly worse. It doesn't offend anybody and all the big brand owners think 'as long as it doesn't offend anyone, we can sell it'. What a dismal way to run a business, pursue a life, look at your face in the mirror each morning.

What our encounters with the small producers has taught us is that to get real flavour and meaningful drinks you have to follow tradition or experiment, be proudly old-fashioned or unnervingly innovative, but do it with passion and integrity.

Actually, the gate was open. Fatheads.

BEER is the answer to everything

(or is it?)

CHAPTER 9: BEER IS THE ANSWER TO EVERYTHING *or is it?*

So here we are at the end of our Grand Tour of the British Isles. We've tasted everything fermented, brewed, distilled or concocted we could along the way and have opened our minds, mouths and taste buds to all facets of the British 'drink experience' (as the marketing people would have it). In fact, we've drunk a lot – in the name of research of course – and now need to draw our conclusions. Many a drink has been suggested to us as the one that speaks for Britain. We park the caravan on the blessed White Cliffs of Dover, lay the candidates out in front of us and remind ourselves what they taste like as we discuss their relative merits.

The object of the exercise was to find the drink that speaks for modern Britain. Which one is it then?

BEER?

Oz: Well, it's obvious isn't it? Beer. Good, true, honest British beer brewed in the proper way. Ale and bitter and bottle-conditioned stuff.

James: I don't think it is. I love it; it's my favourite drink – but the problem is, when we go round the country, that the independent breweries, the hop gardens, the maltsters, they're all disappearing. It's a great drink but it's been intellectualised. It's become a boutique drink for connoisseurs; it's not the everyday drink of the people any more.

Oz: Yes it is, though – it's sprouting all over again. It's being recreated as a wonderful new movement, and it's going to spread like raindrops over a pane of glass so that they eventually become a flood and a lake. If you think that the nation is losing its backbone, beer will bring it back.

WELCOME TO OZ'S BEER LAKE

X no running

X no bombing

X no petting

James: It should, I agree. But if beer is the drink that speaks for Britain, I have to say, and you won't like this, it's lager. It's what people drink. We went to one place that brewed 9 million pints an hour or something. And we don't like it because it's fizzy, cold filth that saps your moral fibre and softens your backbone.

Oz: And it's not an honest pint. I take your point and I have to say that I'm deeply distressed that if we're talking about the drink that speaks for the majority of Britain, it's that fizzy rubbish.

James: But lager isn't a British drink, it's global – a glitzy shallow import that doesn't speak for Britain.

CIDER?
ZIDER?
ZOIDER?

Oz: So what about zider then? The thing is, cider speaks for parts of Britain really well. And maybe we shouldn't be saying we've got to find one drink that speaks for the whole of Britain; maybe we should be fragmenting Britain and saying there are bits of Britain where cider really rules and there are bits of Britain where it's irrelevant.

Sampling the cider at Naish's Cider Farm in the West Country

James: There are bits of Britain where devil worship rules. I don't think we can fragment Britain for the sake of this argument. We want a drink that says, 'This is definitely British because it's a thing that everyone in Britain understands'. It's not cider because cider can't claim that.

Oz: But it represents a whole swathe of the south-west. If we discount that then we have to discount perry, too. Perry's like devil worship.

James: Perry is a minority interest. Most people don't even know what perry is, apart from the people in two villages and three hamlets in the West Country. It's not perry. What about other apple-based things? We've got cider liqueur and cider brandy. I think they're great.

Oz: I do too, but I don't think they're even a British idea. That cider liqueur idea comes from France and the cider brandy, excellent though it is, is sort of a French idea.

James: And I have to be honest, I've never been to anybody's house or to a party where someone's come up to me and said, 'Would you like a cider-based liqueur or brandy?' It just doesn't happen. In your fantasy world of medieval Britain cider liqueur and perry might assume some importance, but in the real world, most people don't know what they are.

WHISKY?

Oz: Ah! Whisky! No, I put my foot down, whisky divides Britain. It doesn't draw it together. The trouble with whisky, I find, is that it's a bit of a fighting drink. It makes nice peaceable people clench their fist and attack strangers.

167

James: The other thing about whisky is that it isn't just made in Scotland. It's also made in Ireland. And in America – out of Bourbon biscuits.

Oz: Scotch, Irish whiskey and American Bourbon are completely different drinks. The original whiskey was made in Ireland, in fact.

James: And whisky is a massive export business. It's something you can experience absolutely everywhere in the world.

Oz: In fact, it's probably easier to get a decent glass of whisky in America than it is in, say, Bournemouth.

James: So it's not whisky.

VODKA?

James: Vodka? Vodka's very popular.

Oz: It's Russian.

James: Well, I know it's an Eastern European idea. But vodka is the basis of a lot of very popular drinks: alcopops, trendy cocktails, vodka with tonic water, and with Coke and other disgusting things like that.

Oz: Basic vodka, the neutral spirit, is the bane of Britain, not the blessing. Basic vodka is like lager: tastes of nothing, gets everyone smashed and makes you go around climbing up lamp-posts and knocking people's heads off. Good vodka is completely different.

James: So is it the drink that speaks for modern Britain?

Oz: No, because most people don't drink good vodka, they drink basic vodka, which is rubbish.

James: OK: basic vodka is the drink that speaks for modern Britain because it is symptomatic of all our ills, it causes problems without giving you anything nice in return. It doesn't even taste of anything.

Oz: So it's like imitation lagers. Imitation vodka, imitation lager, if Britain lacks a backbone, they're probably the reason.

James: I don't think the drink we're looking for is vodka or lager. I think vodka is a fad; also it makes me think of Russia, It makes me think of Nizhny Novgorod.

◄ James: I've just thought of something else that doesn't speak for modern Britain – my homebrew. If Robert Wicks's Churchillian ale was the beer that saved Britain, this is the drink that could destroy it.

GIN?

James: Gin then? Very British.

Oz: Very British. The problem with gin is that the big brands seem to be dumbing it down – which is absolutely horrific in my terms. Gin should be exotic and deeply flavoured and aromatic ... if my favourite gin is James May's gin, I'm afraid the drink that speaks for modern Britain can't be gin.

James's Angelina Jolie gin

James: OK, but you're talking as a drink connoisseur. I'm interested in whether it finds universal favour with the people of this nation. And I don't think it does; although a gin and tonic is one of the truly great drinks and it is very British, it is still slightly stigmatised with the twittering middle-class golf-clubbing Jag-driving blazer with gold buttons type.

Oz: What about building Empire, the Raj, hundreds of thousands of people sitting around ruling people?

James: Oz ... they're gone.   **Oz:** What?

James: The Empire and the Raj. And the people who were sitting around drinking gin and building the empire in places like India were no more than about 20,000 people in total. The honest toiling people of Britain were building steam engines and canals and bridges and battleships. They weren't sitting around drinking a gin and tonic.

Oz: What were they drinking, then? I'll tell you: India Pale Ale. Now that's a good drink.

James: Yes, but they don't drink it now.

WINE?

James: Now this next one is going to cause a bit of a row. The hop gardens have gone, the vineyards are coming in. The climate favours them. The soil is good, the chalk is good, the slope is good, the late summer sun is good, our position in terms of latitude on the Earth is good, the French are interested in our land. Is wine the drink?

Three Choirs Vineyard
in Gloucestershire

Oz: We are sitting here on the soil that is going to make Britain great as a wine-producing nation. This is the band of cretaceous chalk that runs as the North Downs and the South Downs from the Dover cliffs right the way down to Portland Bill and Weymouth. It's exactly the same soil as the Champagne boys use — and the people in Chablis and the people in Sancerre and Cognac.

James: Exactly. That's exactly why it isn't the drink that defines modern Britain. Drinking wine says a lot about modern Britain, but the wine we make doesn't. And the fact is that the great wines of France will remain the great wines of France for a very long time. And this brings me rather neatly to that great conceit, English sparkling wine.

Oz: It's very good.

James: Yes, but it isn't the drink that speaks for modern Britain and the reason is that Champagne and the imitations of Champagne are nothing to do with drinking any more. It is purely a status symbol, an expression of poshness, it's an off-the-peg gift for celebrations when people pass their driving test, have a baby, get married, fill in their tax return. Very few people are interested in the drink Champagne, they are interested in the cult of Champagne, in the luxury goods experience of Champagne, and, as we've seen, the English ones still aren't as nice as the Californian ones.

Oz: If you'd just stop talking for a minute, I'd say I agree with you. Champagne is just an image. What you're holding in your hand is not Champagne. It's English sparkling wine, it's different. We drink it because we love the idea of having our own fabulous sparkling wine — and it is world class. It doesn't speak for England yet, but it will.

James: I disagree.

Oz: In 20 or 30 years' time all of these English shires are going to be covered in vineyards, I'm convinced of it, and we're going to be fantastically proud of them and drink their wine day in day out.

James: But it's still not a uniquely British experience. You'll still get wine in France and Italy and Spain and California and Germany and Romania and Germany and ... Yorkshire.

Oz: Like there is beer in all of those countries, and with the exception of Germany and California it's all rubbish.

James: Yes, but our beer is not the nation's drink any more; it's become, let's be honest, slightly poncy. You and I sit around talking about it. Stout – now there's a question.

STOUT?

Oz: The thing about stout is that it claims to speak for one part of the British Isles, Ireland. But does it? I don't think so. I think because of the appallingly monopolistic nature of stout brewing in Ireland, the people of Ireland haven't got any choice. So stout could be the drink that speaks for one part of the British Isles but it doesn't, because there's no free will involved.

James: I think the stout you are talking about – the one we can't mention...

Oz: The stout that dare not speak its name...

James: I think it has become more of a badge than a drink. It's become a cliché.

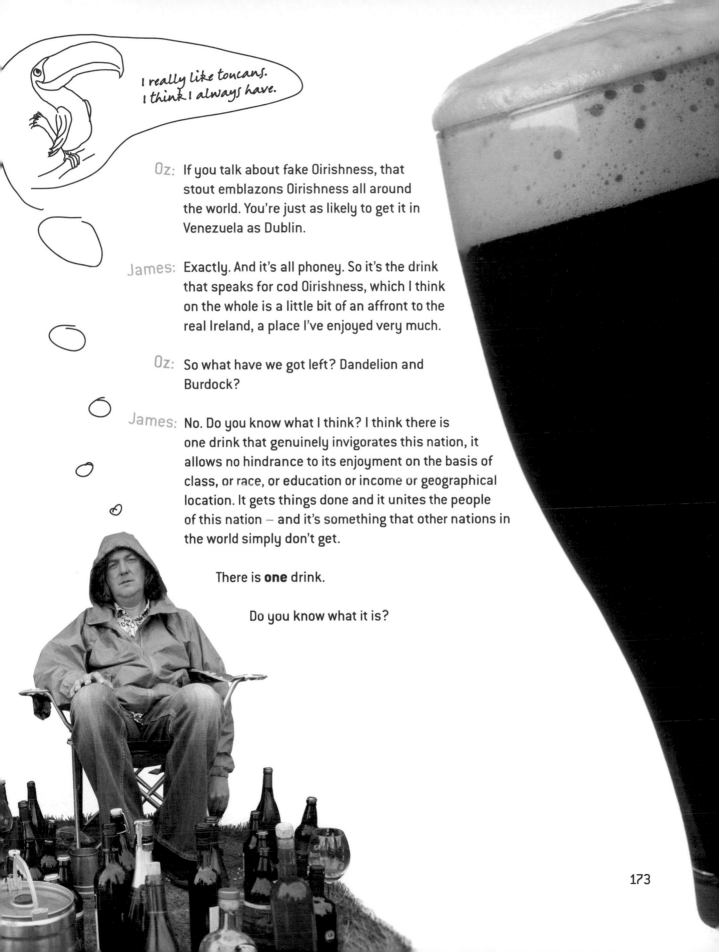

I really like toucans. I think I always have.

Oz: If you talk about fake Oirishness, that stout emblazons Oirishness all around the world. You're just as likely to get it in Venezuela as Dublin.

James: Exactly. And it's all phoney. So it's the drink that speaks for cod Oirishness, which I think on the whole is a little bit of an affront to the real Ireland, a place I've enjoyed very much.

Oz: So what have we got left? Dandelion and Burdock?

James: No. Do you know what I think? I think there is one drink that genuinely invigorates this nation, it allows no hindrance to its enjoyment on the basis of class, or race, or education or income or geographical location. It gets things done and it unites the people of this nation — and it's something that other nations in the world simply don't get.

There is **one** drink.

Do you know what it is?

James: It's a cup of tea. Good old builders' tea. Tea is the drink that speaks for modern Britain.

Oz: Do you want one?

James: I'd love one. Are you mashing?

Oz: I'm mashing. So we've been round these British Isles, tasted everything we could lay our hands on and we come back to the one drink that no other country in the world can make right. You go abroad certain in the knowledge that you won't get a decent cuppa until you hit these blessed shores again.

James: Aye — and remember to put the milk in first. Fathead.

James's Tea Commandments

1   For a given tea, the loose-leaf version will always taste better than the bags

2   For a given tea, the bag version will block your sink up a lot less than the loose leaves

3   Tea made in a pot tastes better than tea made in the cup

4   The teapot should always be heated first

5   Metal teapots are OK, but not if the knob's fallen off the lid

6   Dripping tea pots are often caused by a build-up of tea stain under the spout, for complicated molecular reasons

7   Excess air in the pot spoils the flavour for some reason. Don't half-fill an oversized pot

8   Tea cosies do make a difference, but may not be worth the social stigma, especially if they feature pictures of cats

9   Thin cups make tea taste better than thick ones

10 Cardboard cups are not acceptable

11 The milk should go in the cup first

12 Tea is not tea if it doesn't have tea in it, viz 'peppermint tea'

13 Tea made by James May arrives around one hour before tea made by Oz Clarke

14 Lapsang Souchong is rubbish

15 Coffee is the work of Satan

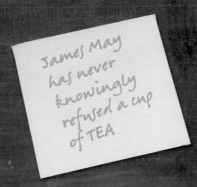

James May has never knowingly refused a cup of TEA

British drinks

finding out more

ancient →

4000BC: Ancient cultures start cultivating crops, brewing beer and fermenting wine.

100BC: Romans arrive in Britain and plant vines; Northamptonshire was a leading centre for viticulture. Ale-drinking culture already well established. The Romans introduce the first inns, or tabernae, as they were known, where wine was sold; the Anglo-Saxons set up alehouses, forerunners of the modern-day pub, in and around domestic dwellings.

wine versus ale debate begins

Late 1600s: Commercial ('common') breweries begin to take the place of home brewhouses, where beer was made to be consumed on the premises. By the end of the century the common breweries brew almost all British beer.

1690: The Government allows unlicensed distilling and imposes a heavy duty on imported spirits. Gin-shops spring up throughout England.

1066: Normans arrive. Wine and cider become the drinks of choice.

410AD: Romans leave Britain – first theme pub established in celebration.

medieval →

c1520: The first hops grown in south-east England.

1677: First reference to 'stout', meaning 'strong beer'.

1694: Taxes on beer raised, so gin becomes cheaper than beer.

1400s: Hopped beer imported from Holland.

Elizabethan →

1405: First written record of whiskey in Ireland. However, it is thought that Irish monks had been distilling whiskey for several centuries before this. First documented in Scotland in 1494.

Late 1500s: Coal furnaces invented in Britain; the glassmaking industry produces the first really strong glass bottles for wine and cider.

1437: Brewers' Company in the City of London granted a royal charter by Henry VI. They initially opposed the use of hops, or 'the wicked weed'.

1572: Gin, flavoured with juniper, created in the Netherlands. First used as a medicine, to treat stomach and kidney disorders, gallstones, lumbago and gout, gin soon gained popularity as a social drink.

1598: John Stow records that 26 London breweries are producing 648,900 barrels a year.

I prescribe ... GIN!

x 648,900

1703: Methuen Treaty gives Portuguese wines preferential duties over French wines. The English become a main consumer of port.

1751: Gin Act legislates to control the sale of gin through licensed public houses.

1830: Beerhouse Act abolishes tax on beer and frees up the selling of beer, ale and cider, allowing pubs to open from 4am to 10pm. Forty thousand new pubs open in the next 10 years.

2008: James May brews his first pint and distils his first gin. Pubs closing at the rate of 36 a week. Any connection?

1995: 'Alcopops' – ready-mixed soft drinks containing alcohol – introduced.

1992: English wine production peaks at 3.5 million bottles (15 years later production averages just over 2 million bottles).

1948: 'Dimple' pint glass appears in British pubs; it's ideal for appreciating the amber colour of draught bitter.

1928: 'Guinness is good for you' is the slogan of the first modern beer advertising campaign.

georgian

1740s: Because it is so cheap, gin is excessively popular with the poor, most of whom were off their heads all week long. Of the 15,000 drinking establishments in London, more than half are gin-shops.

1849: The term 'alcoholism' is coined by the Swedish physician Magnus Huss to describe the adverse effects of continual excessive alcohol consumption.

victorian

1878: Acreage of hops in England reaches its peak of 72,000 acres.

20th century

1765: James Watt invents the steam engine. Eventually, this allows brewers to make greater quantities of beer, as human power is no longer a limiting factor.

1832: Joseph Livesey starts his Temperance Movement in Preston, requiring followers to sign a pledge of total abstinence. The following year the term teetotal is derived from a speech by Richard Turner, a follower of Livesey.

1836: 12 main London brewers produce 2.2 million barrels.

1847: Band of Hope founded in Leeds, to save working class children from the perils of drink. Members had to pledge to abstain 'from all liquors of an intoxicating quality, whether ale, porter, wine or ardent spirits, except as medicine'.

1870s: Refrigeration machines introduced, allowing larger breweries to produce beer all year round (previously many of them had ceased brewing during the summer). Yeast is very sensitive to temperature, and if a beer was produced during summer, the yeast might not be able to complete the fermentation and the beer would sour. Most brewers would make enough beer during winter to last through the summer, and store it in underground cellars to protect it from the heat.

1914: In an attempt to curb excessive drinking and increase wartime productivity, the Defence of the Realm Act restricts pub opening hours to midday to 2.30pm and 6.30 to 9.30pm.

now!

x 1,200,000

179

BRITISH BEER STYLES

Mild is one of the oldest beer styles. It is usually dark brown, though it can be bronze in colour, and often tastes lightly malty, fruity, nutty, even slightly sweet. It has a typical alcohol content of around 3% to 3.5%, though some microbreweries produce considerably stronger versions, which are enjoying renewed success in the real ale market.

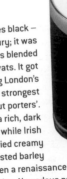

Porter is a dark beer – sometimes black – dating from the early 18th century; it was originally a blend of old and young ales blended together in vast wooden 'tuns' or vats. It got its name from its popularity among London's market porters. **Stout** derives from the strongest porters, which were known as 'stout porters'. British stouts and porters shared a rich, dark malt character and hop bitterness, while Irish stouts were darker still and married creamy depth with a powerful burnt roasted barley bitterness. There has recently been a renaissance of stout and porter production among craft breweries. Nowadays porters usually have around 4% to 6% alcohol, and stouts from 4% to 8%.

Pale ale is a clear, amber or copper-coloured beer that became popular in the early 19th century when consumers preferred it to the dark, cloudy ales and porters of the time. **India Pale Ale (IPA)** was originally a strong, well-hopped ale that would weather the long sea journey from Blighty to India without going off. The high hop and alcohol content allowed IPA to resist the microbes that can make beer go sour and stale. Juicy malt flavours, a strong hoppy bitterness and higher alcohol content marked IPAs from pale ales. Nowadays many beers labelled IPA are indistinguishable from other pale ales or bitters. There are exceptions though, and this style has gained favour with microbreweries worldwide. The best examples today are made in the USA, that well-known repository of British colonial pride.

Old ales can be dark or light in colour, though they usually tend to be ruby or dark brown. The main characteristic of an old ale is the lengthy term of maturation, usually in bottles, and the marvellous 'winey' depth of flavour this imparts. Independent breweries still produce small amounts, if only to keep their Head Brewer happy. Draught versions may be called winter warmers, and range from 4% to 6.5% alcohol.

Bitter grew out of the 19th-century taste for pale ales, and appeared as brewers began to make beers that could be served after a short storage period in pubs: so-called 'running beers'. Before then, most beers were matured in huge vats for months. Most bitter has an alcohol content of between 3.5% and 5%, and is amber or copper-coloured. 'Best' is generally a brewery's stronger version of bitter, over 4% alcohol content, and Special or Extra Strong Bitter (ESB) has 5% alcohol or more. Hops give bitter its characteristic aroma and bite.

Barley wine originated in England in the 18th century. It is a strong ale – between 8% and 12 % alcohol – which, in days of yore, when conflict with the French meant drinking Bordeaux was a no-no, was sometimes substituted for wine. Because of its high alcohol and hop content, barley wine can be stored in its bottle for years, like wine, and often has strong sweet and bitter notes.

Scottish beers were traditionally sweeter, darker and less heavily hopped than English ales. This is changing with the new generation of craft brewers. In the 19th century, Scottish ales were taxed by the 'shilling' (there were 20 shillings to the pound for those of you under about 50 years of age), according to their strength, and styles ranged from the light 60/- (that's the old shilling sign), through 80/-, a full, round 'export' style, to 'Wee Heavy' or 90/-, a strong ale similar to a barley wine.

Golden ales are thirstquenching beers, pale in colour and served cool. Their strength ranges from 3.5% to over 5%. Developed in the 1980s as a way of attracting custom from the dominating keg lager brands, these ales have a delicate juicy flavour, often with a citrus tang imparted by aromatic hops.

BEER GLOSSARY

Alcohol What you get by fermenting sugars with yeast. Virtually any kind of fruit or grain will ferment to some extent. Grapes, apples and barley are the most successful.

ABV (alcohol by volume) The worldwide standard for measuring a drink's alcohol content. The measure of the amount of space the alcohol in a drink takes up as a percentage of total volume.

Ale In the 15th and 16th centuries the term was used to distinguish the unhopped fermented grain drink from the hopped drink known as beer. Now used to mean beer made with a 'top-fermenting' strain of yeast – one that works at the top of the fermentation tank – as opposed to lager, which is made with 'bottom-fermenting' yeast. Favoured drink of rotund, bearded folk, and Oz Clarke.

Barley The grain normally used to make beer. God's gift to mankind, along with the grape. And yeast. And spam.

Barrel In Britain, a beer barrel holds 36 gallons (163 litres).

Bitterness The sharp flavour imparted by hops in beer, which offsets the sweetness provided by malts. The feeling engendered by coming second in a beer-judging contest, where there are only two entries – Oz and James (see page 123).

Body The 'thickness' of a beer in your mouth. Dark, malty beers, like stout or porter, are usually more 'full-bodied' than 'thin-bodied' pale beers like lager or golden ale.

Bottle conditioning The secondary fermentation that occurs when more yeast and sugars are added to the beer just before bottling. Bottle conditioning can give a beer a higher alcoholic content than cask conditioning, and allows it to be aged. Oz Clarke is, therefore, well 'bottle conditioned'.

Cask conditioning Proper beer! Rather than being filtered and pasteurised and stored in a pressurised keg, cask-conditioned beer is kept in a cask with its yeast. A slight secondary fermentation gives real ale its distinctive character and flavour. Cask-conditioned beers keep for a shorter time than keg beers, but taste much better.

Draught beer Beers dispensed from casks or kegs, rather than from bottles. What you get in pubs.

Dry hopping Adding extra hops to a beer in barrel or tank to give heady, 'hoppy' flavours and aromas without affecting the bitterness of the beer.

Fermentation The conversion of sugars to alcohol and carbon dioxide by yeast.

Hops The flower of the female hop plant, and usually one of the four essential ingredients of beer, along with water, malt and yeast. Hops add bitterness, flavour and aroma to beer, and have preservative qualities.

Keg beer Keg beer is what we're too commonly used to drinking in pubs and bars. The keg is a sealed metal container in which the conditioning of the beer has been completed in the brewery, including pasteurisation of the beer to make it sterile. The beer, though lacking in character and flavour, is ready to drink and has a comparatively long shelf life. Extra carbon dioxide and sometimes nitrogen are pumped into the beer to give it its distinctive sharp fizz and head. Most bottled or canned beers and lagers are also produced in this way.

Lager A beer made with 'bottom-fermenting' strains of yeast, meaning that the yeast works at the bottom of the fermentation tank. Real lagers are brewed and aged for longer than ales and at colder temperatures, and drunk by jovial continentals. Imitation 'bastard' lagers are drunk by idiots in Britain.

Malt One of the main ingredients of beer. Malt is barley that has been 'tricked' into germinating so its sugars become accessible for fermentation.

Mash/mashing The process whereby malt is mixed with water, extracting fermentable sugars from the malts. This creates the 'wort' – the liquid malt extract ready for fermentation.

Mash tun The vessel used for 'mashing'. Dustbin, plastic bucket or bathtub are other terms.

Pasteurisation Heating of beer to 60-79°C/140-174°F to stop further microbiological action. Mucks up the flavour of the beer like nobody's business. Ineptly done, it makes the beer taste like burnt caramel spilt on a damp, dirty carpet in a student squat.

Wort (pronounced 'wert') The liquid malt extract, created by 'mashing', that is ready for the fermentation tank, where yeast will be added. A facial disfigurement, popular in the Middle Ages.

Yeast Fungus used to convert the sugars in malt into alcohol and carbon dioxide. *Saccharomyces cerevisiae* is the top-fermenting yeast used to make ales, while *Saccharomyces carlsbergensis* is used to make bottom-fermenting lagers.

Zymurgy The science of fermentation in brewing. A term used to fill in awkward gaps in a crossword.

CAMRA
The Campaign for Real Ale, founded in 1971, has more than 94,000 members; it campaigns for real ale, real pubs and consumer rights, publishes books and promotes beer festivals, where you can try hundreds of different beers. The CAMRA website includes a calendar of beer festivals throughout the UK. www.camra.org.uk

Recent CAMRA research found that only one in three British drinkers had tried real ale – but 69% had drunk lager and 78% had tasted wine. So, which drink speaks for Britain?

The vineyard at Three Choirs, Gloucestershire.
(Hey, it could almost pass for a Roman villa.)

A potted history

The Romans brought vines to England, and they certainly had a crack at growing their own wine to supplement what they imported from their homeland. When the Romans withdrew at the beginning of the fifth century, the Dark Ages descended and it was left to the monasteries to uphold the tradition of growing grapes and making wine, which was an important part of the Christian ritual. English wine production got a boost when the Normans arrived in 1066, bringing with them monks who had experience of winemaking, and by the late 11th century (according to *Domesday Book*) there were 40 vineyards here. But when Henry II married Eleanor of Aquitaine in 1152, we English started our extended love affair with the wines of Bordeaux and our native wine production started to decline. Henry VIII delivered the *coup de grâce* to our already terminally ill wine 'industry' in 1536 with the Dissolution of the Monasteries, where the only remaining vineyards had survived.

Over the next four centuries only a few brave souls – who also happened to be wealthy landowners – dipped their toes into the chilly waters of English (and Welsh) winemaking. The Marquess of Bute planted a three-acre vineyard at Castle Coch near Cardiff in 1875 and achieved some success until just before World War I.

Today's renaissance began in the 1950s with experimental plantings in Surrey and Kent, and small commercial vineyards in Sussex and Hampshire. The expansion of vineyards gradually gained momentum throughout the 1960s and 70s, peaking in the mid-1990s. In 2007 there were around 100 wineries in the UK, with about 2400 acres (1000 hectares) of vines. These vines produce roughly 2 million bottles annually.

Wine styles

In the 1970s, German Liebfraumilch – light, sweetish and low in alcohol – was a bestseller in the UK; English wineries catered for popular taste with German-style whites and consumers didn't have a problem if they were labelled Reichensteiner, Huxelrebe or Müller-Thurgau. (Or Rosencrantz and Guildenstern.)

Since the 1980s consumers have demanded drier wines. Producers had gained expertise in a variety of styles, both red and white, and began using oak barrels to mature their wines. They also make some pretty good rosé, which is great news as the market for pink wine is booming.

Along the way, English wine producers made the happy discovery that they could make truly excellent sparkling wine; fizz now accounts for 15% (and rising) of UK wine production.

Leventhorpe wine. It's from Yorkshire, don't you know.

Label lore

Since 2004, English and Welsh wines have been subject to a European-approved labelling scheme, approximating to the Appellation Contrôlée system in France. Here's how it works:

English (or Welsh) Vineyards Quality Wine PSR (Produced in a Specific Region) The top stuff. The grapes must be 100% from the stated region, yield is limited, the wine is analysed in a laboratory and assessed by an official tasting panel.

English (or Welsh) Regional Wine Usually pretty good. 85% of the grapes must come from the stated region, and the wine must be approved by an official tasting panel.

UK Table Wine May be quite drinkable, or suitable only for cleaning paintbrushes. The only requirement is that the grapes are grown in the UK.

British wine Don't touch it. Alcoholic sugar water, made from imported grapes or concentrated grape juice. Nasty.

VINEYARDS AND WINERIES

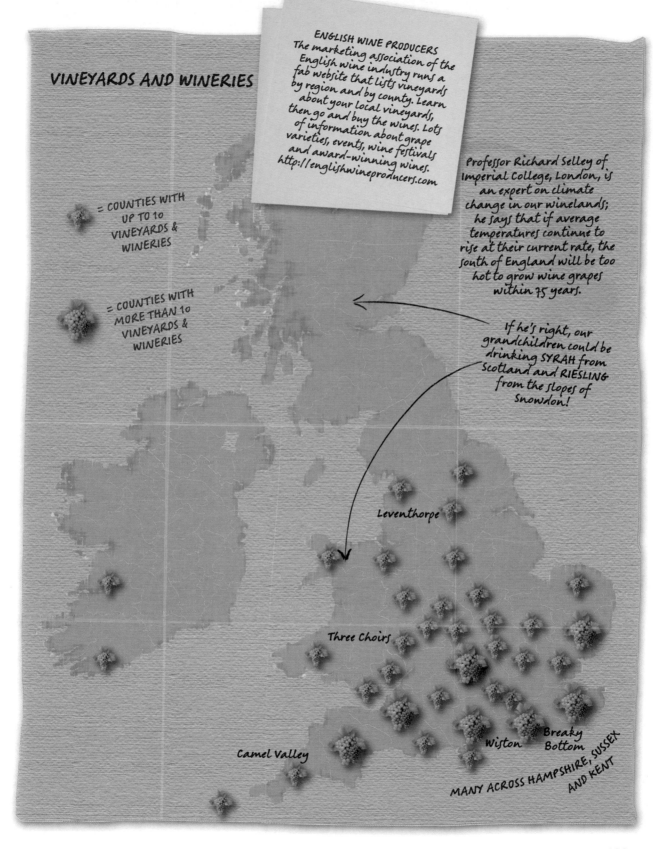

= COUNTIES WITH UP TO 10 VINEYARDS & WINERIES

= COUNTIES WITH MORE THAN 10 VINEYARDS & WINERIES

ENGLISH WINE PRODUCERS
The marketing association of the English wine industry runs a fab website that lists vineyards by region and by county. Learn about your local vineyards, then go and buy the wines. Lots of information about grape varieties, events, wine festivals and award-winning wines.
http://englishwineproducers.com

Professor Richard Selley of Imperial College, London, is an expert on climate change in our winelands; he says that if average temperatures continue to rise at their current rate, the south of England will be too hot to grow wine grapes within 75 years.

If he's right, our grandchildren could be drinking SYRAH from Scotland and RIESLING from the slopes of Snowdon!

Leventhorpe

Three Choirs

Wiston

Breaky Bottom

Camel Valley

MANY ACROSS HAMPSHIRE, SUSSEX AND KENT

A BLUFFER'S GUIDE TO WHISKY

Scotch whisky must be distilled and matured – for a minimum of three years in oak casks – in Scotland.

Single malt is the product of a single distillery, using malted barley as the only grain ingredient. It must be made in pot stills and is usually matured in cask for between eight and 20 years.

Blended malt, also known as vatted malt or pure malt, is a blend of single malt whiskies, distilled at more than one distillery.

Irish whiskey is traditionally made in a pot still from a mixture of malted and unmalted barley, oats and wheat. Peat is not generally used in the malting and the style is traditionally smooth and mellow. **Pure pot still whiskey** is a distinctive Irish product made from 100 per cent barley, both malted and unmalted, distilled in a pot still. **Poteen** (aka **poitin**) is named after the small pot still in which it is made, from malted barley, molasses or potatoes. It is very strong (up to 95% alcohol by volume) and in 1661 the English made it illegal – which added to the fun for many Irish drinkers. Raids by the Garda (Irish police) have reduced the number of illicit stills, and commercial brands have been legalized since 1997.

Grain whisky is made from a mixture of malted barley and unmalted cereal grains such as wheat and corn (maize). It is distilled in a patent still – developed in 1831 and also known as a Coffey still, after its inventor. Generally milder in flavour than malt whisky, it is the basis for **Blended Scotch** (blended with different malt whiskies to create a consistent product), but can also be sold as **Single grain Scotch** whisky (the product of one distillery), enjoyed for its subtle flavour.

Aged whisky – when a bottle carries an age statement (e.g. 12 years old) all the whisky in the bottle must have matured in the cask for at least that amount of time.

Single malt whisky

For connoisseurs, whisky varies as much as wine, depending not only on where it is made, but also on its strength, how old it is and the cask or casks in which it has been matured – principally ex-sherry and ex-Bourbon casks. Some whiskies are 'finished' (a second, shorter period of maturation) in a different cask, such as port, wine or rum.

Highland – the largest region, with the widest range of styles. Whiskies from the north may be spicy, those from the east and centre are often fruity and those made near the sea can have a salty tang.

Speyside – often considered the most delicate and complex of whiskies, with a refined smokiness.

Islay – peaty, smoky, even seaweedy.

Campbeltown – full-bodied, robust, smoky, with the tang of the sea.

Lowland – the lightest of the malts in both colour and weight, sometimes grassy or floral, with a dry finish.

Websites for more information:

The Scotch Malt Whisky Society, www.smws.co.uk
The Scotch Whisky Association, www.scotch-whisky.org.uk
Whisky Classified, www.whiskyclassified.com

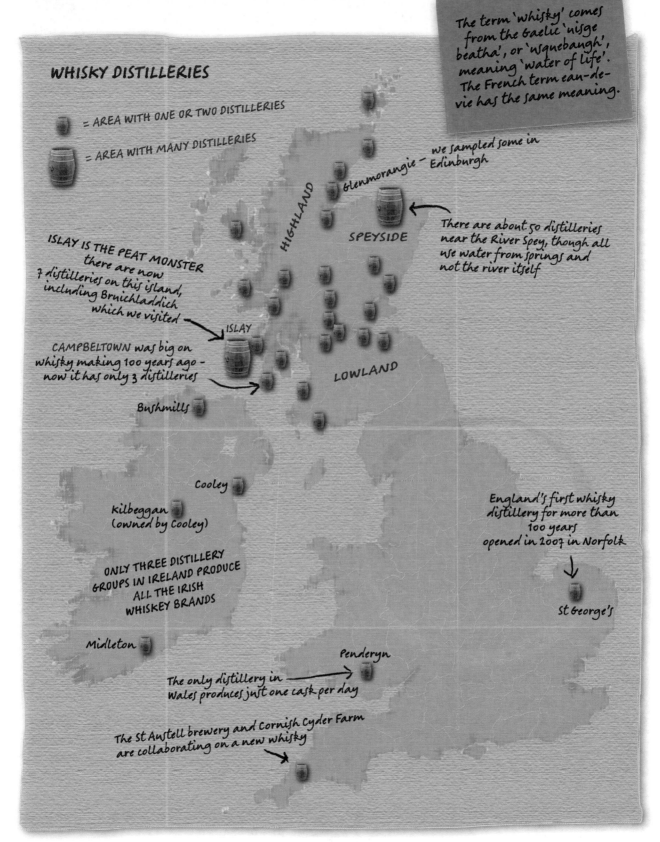

WHISKY DISTILLERIES

= AREA WITH ONE OR TWO DISTILLERIES

= AREA WITH MANY DISTILLERIES

The term 'whisky' comes from the Gaelic 'uisge beatha', or 'usquebaugh', meaning 'water of life'. The French term eau-de-vie has the same meaning.

Glenmorangie – we sampled some in Edinburgh

HIGHLAND

SPEYSIDE

There are about 50 distilleries near the River Spey, though all use water from springs and not the river itself

ISLAY IS THE PEAT MONSTER there are now 7 distilleries on this island, including Bruichladdich which we visited

ISLAY

CAMPBELTOWN was big on whisky making 100 years ago - now it has only 3 distilleries

LOWLAND

Bushmills

Cooley

Kilbeggan (owned by Cooley)

ONLY THREE DISTILLERY GROUPS IN IRELAND PRODUCE ALL THE IRISH WHISKEY BRANDS

England's first whisky distillery for more than 100 years opened in 2007 in Norfolk

St George's

Midleton

Penderyn

The only distillery in Wales produces just one cask per day

The St Austell brewery and Cornish Cyder Farm are collaborating on a new whisky

185

CIDER AND SUCHLIKE

WHAT IS CIDER, REALLY?

The Campaign for Real Ale (CAMRA) took an interest in 'real' cider when this traditional drink was seen to be going the way of keg beer — sweetened, pasteurised, artificially preserved and carbonated. So, real cider (or perry) is made from the juice of freshly pressed fruit, with nothing added and nothing taken away.

AND SCRUMPY?

Scrumpy has no fixed definition; originally it meant cider made from windfalls, or 'scrumps'. Most people think of it as rough, cloudy, strong cider, and it can mean young cider — though some cidermakers use the term for their finest ciders.

APPLES AND PEARS

There are hundreds of varieties of apples and pears that can be used to make cider and perry. The drinks are usually made from a blend of different varieties, so you don't need to know your Dunkerton from your Dabinett, but a little knowledge can be a wonderful thing.

Cider sites
* The Cider Museum, Hereford
  www.cidermuseum.co.uk
* Middle Farm, www.middlefarm.com
  A working farm near Lewes in East Sussex that welcomes visitors — and houses the National Collection of Cider and Perry: more than 100 draught ciders and perries (including their own Pookhill Cider).
* National Association of Cider Makers (NACM), www.cideruk.com
* Old Scrump's Cider House
  www.ciderandperry.co.uk
  A fabulous website covering everything you ever wanted to know about cider and perry, including contact information for the 100 or so craft makers in the UK, and a list of cider festivals around the country.
* South-West of England Cider Makers Association, www.tinyurl.com.pylmg
* Three Counties Cider and Perry Association
  www.thethreecountiesciderandperryassociation.co.uk
* The Welsh Perry and Cider Society
  www.welshcider.co.uk

SOME CIDER APPLES

Ashton Brown Jersey
Brown Snout
Collington Big Bitters
Dabinett
Dunkerton Late Sweet
Foxwhelp
Kingston Black
Michelin
Redstreak
Stoke Red
Tom Putt
Tremlett's Bitter
Vileberie (aka Villebery, Vilbery)
Yarlington Mill

SOME PERRY PEARS WERE MENTIONED IN CHAPTER 6

Anorak's corner
* 45% of the apples grown in the UK are used for cidermaking.
* Between 1995 and 2006, more than two million cider apple trees were planted.
* The UK produces more than 130 million gallons (6 million hectolitres) of cider a year — and more than 1,300 million gallons (60 million hectolitres) of beer.

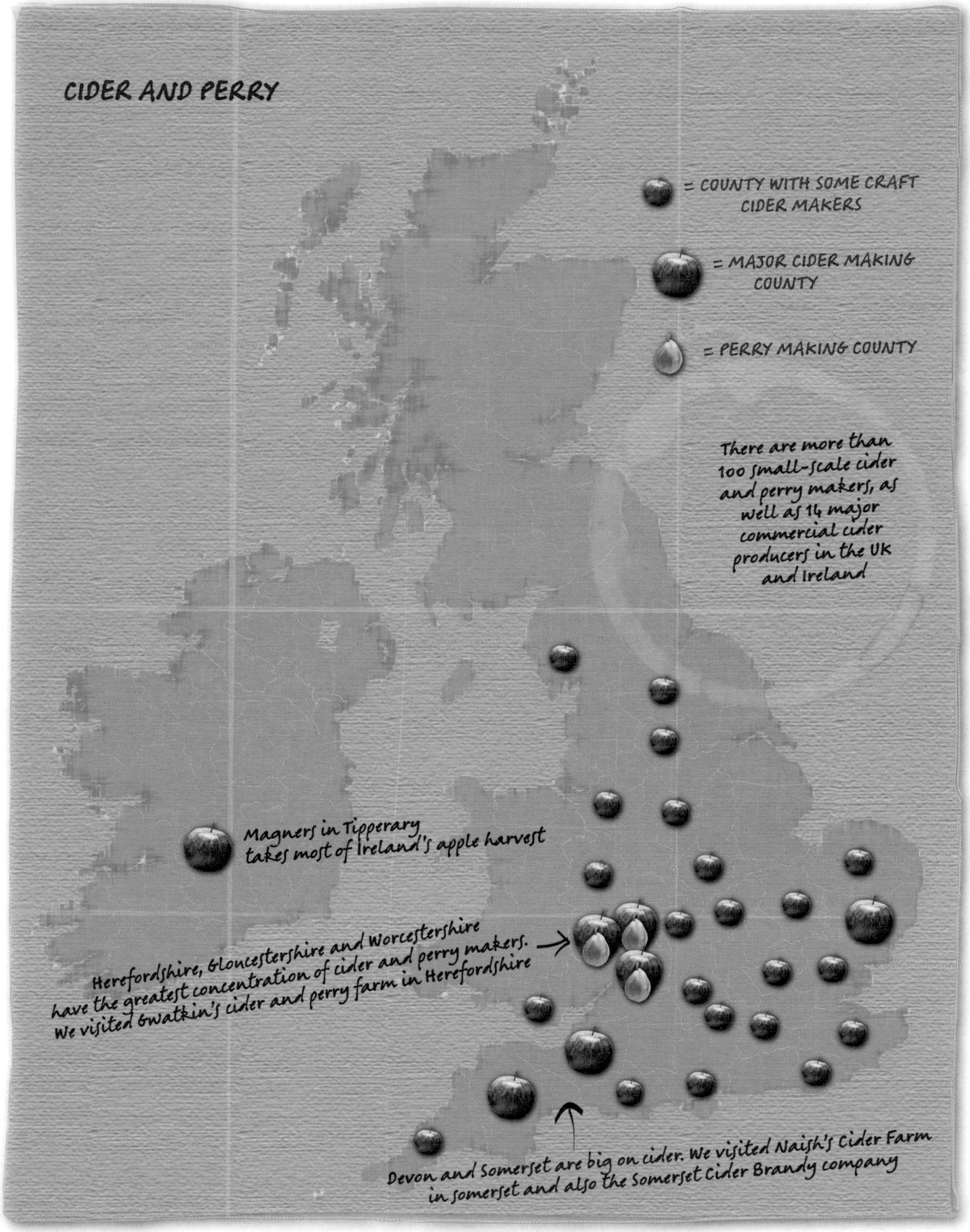

CIDER AND PERRY
= COUNTY WITH SOME CRAFT CIDER MAKERS
= MAJOR CIDER MAKING COUNTY
= PERRY MAKING COUNTY
There are more than 100 small-scale cider and perry makers, as well as 14 major commercial cider producers in the UK and Ireland
Magners in Tipperary takes most of Ireland's apple harvest
Herefordshire, Gloucestershire and Worcestershire have the greatest concentration of cider and perry makers. We visited Gwatkin's cider and perry farm in Herefordshire
Devon and Somerset are big on cider. We visited Naish's Cider Farm in Somerset and also the Somerset Cider Brandy company

DRAMATIS PERSONAE

SPRITES AND CREW

Michael 'Rommell' Davies, Hannah Gibson, Ben Hewish,
Maria Morley, James Pursey, Sam Rogers, Ian Salvage,
Vivia Togneri

OUR DRINK HEROES

Chapter 1

Thomas Fawcett & Sons
James Fawcett
www.fawcett-maltsters.co.uk

Thornbridge Brewery
Stef Cosani and Kelly Ryan
www.thornbridgebrewery.
co.uk

Chapter 2

Prospect Brewery
Patsy Slevin
www.prospectbrewery.com

Leventhorpe Vineyard
George Bowden
Bullerthorpe Lane
Woodlesford
Leeds, West Yorkshire
LS26 8AF
Telephone: 0113 288 9088
Fax: 0113 266 7892

**Trans-Pennine Rail Ale
Trail**
West Riding Refreshment Rooms
Dewsbury station
Michael Field, Sarah Barnes
www.imissedthetrain.com/west

The Ship Inn
Low Newton by the Sea
Northumberland
Tel: 01665 576262
Christine, Hannah, Michael

Chapter 3

Glenmorangie
Rachel Barrie
www.glenmorangie.com

BrewDog
Martin Dickie and
James Watt
www.brewdog.com

New Alloa Brewery
Bruce and Scott Williams
www.williamsbrosbrew.com
www.fraoch.com

**Bruichladdich
Distillery**
Mark Reynier
Jim McEwan
www.bruichladdich.com

Chapter 4

Guinness Brewery
Fergal Murray
www.guinness-storehouse.
com

**Carlow Brewing
Company**
www.carlowbrewing.com

Bull and Castle
www.bullandcastle.ie

Chapter 5

Worthington's
Steve Wellington
www.worthingtons
whiteshield.com

Windsor Castle Inn
Chris and John Sadler
www.windsorcastle
brewery.com

Chapter 6

**Tyrrells/Williams
Chase Distillery**
Will Chase
James Baxter
www.tyrrellspotatochips.
co.uk
www.williamschasedistillery.
com

Gwatkin Cider Company
Denis Gwatkin
Moorhampton Park Farm
Abbeydore
Hereford HR2 0AL
Tel: 01981 550258
Free admission to the farm –
but ring to confirm

Three Choirs Vineyard
Martin Fowke
Thomas Shaw
www.three-choirs-
vineyards.co.uk

Chapter 7

Naish's Cider Farm
The lovely Frank Naish
and Paul Chant
They don't have a
website (well, they only
got electricity in 2003)
but you can call on
01749 890260 to arrange
a visit.

**The Somerset Cider
Brandy Company**
Julian Temperley
www.ciderbrandy.co.uk

Camel Valley Vineyard
Sam and Bob Lindo
www.camelvalley.com

Plymouth Gin
www.plymouthgin.com

Chapter 8

**Wiston Estate
Winery**
Dermot Sugrue
07887 507216
www.
winebehindthelabel.
com/
DermotsDiaryX.htm

Breaky Bottom Vineyard
Peter Hall
www.breaky
bottom.co.uk

Westerham Brewery
Robert Wicks
www.westerhambrewery.co.uk

Ian Strang
Little Scotney Farm
Lamberhurst
Tunbridge Wells
Kent TN3 8JN

*Thank you to
everyone else we
met along the
way as well...*

GREAT BRITISH WEBSITES
Common Ground:
www.england-in-particular.info
The Gin and Vodka Association:
www.ginvodka.org
British Beer and Pub Association:
www.beerandpub.com

INDEX

PICTURE CREDITS

ACoRP (THE ASSOCIATION OF COMMUNITY RAIL PARTNERSHIPS): Train and station on Rail Ale Trail p48

ALAMY: Lovely Day for a Guinness poster p77

ANOVA BOOKS (photographer Gary Moyes): Oz and James pp7, 10, 15, Oz's head pp17, 19, 25, 30, 65, 72, 95, James May p47, 154; cidermaking engraving by Christopher Wormell (from *English Country Traditions*, published in 1990 by Pavilion, an imprint of Anova Books)

BREAKY BOTTOM VINEYARD: Landscape, bottles and portrait of Peter Hall p155

BRUICHLADDICH: Casks at Bruichladdich p67, equipment p69, bottles 70, landscape p72, beach images p73, bottle p184, Jim McEwan at Bruichladdich p188

CAMEL VALLEY VINEYARD: Grape harvest and wine bottles p138

COMPASS BOX: Hedonism bottle p184

GETTY IMAGES: Richard Burton p88

GLENMORANGIE DISTILLERY: Bottle pp56–7

JAMES MAY: Hand-drawn graph p102

LEVENTHORPE VINEYARD: George Bowden p42 (image used in photomontage), vineyard sign p43, vineyard p44

MARY EVANS PICTURE LIBRARY: Burton in 1840 p93 (used in joke postcard photomontage), wassailing p130

 MICHELIN et Cie, 2008, Authorisation No GB0810007. Extract from map 798: Permission to reproduce Michelin maps within the photomontages on pp14, 34, 54, 76, 90, 108, 126, 148

PROSPECT BREWERY: Artworks pp38–9

JAMES PURSEY: barley page 3, page 4 (both), on cliff at Dover p8, Rolls and caravan p11, in barley field p16, lying in malt p23, car and at Thornbridge p27, Thornbridge tasting p29, car p36, garden p40, homebrewing in caravan p40, with George Bowden at Leventhorpe p44, eating deep fried food p60, at Bruichladdich p73, Oz and James outside pub p74, James pulling pint p79, outside pub p82, car and caravan p96, under grey skies p109, kneeling on grass p122, Frank Naish p131, caravan tilted p143, caravan mess p145, Wiston landscape pp146–7, car and caravan p149, at Wiston pp150–1, Coquard press p153, blind tasting at Breaky Bottom p157 (above right, below left), Oz and James climbing over Westerham gate p161, at white cliffs of Dover pp162–3, car and caravan p178, images for Thornbridge Brewery, Leventhorpe Vineyard, Glenmorangie tasting and Wiston Estate pp188–9

RDF MEDIA: beach at sunset page 1, all images page 2, grapes and apples page 3, Oz and James with Morris men p8, in front of caravan, p9, Spirit of Ecstasy and washing Rolls p11, Maltkiln Lane sign p12, James's head p19, James Fawcett and James May p21, Fawcett's truck p22, pint on car pp32–3, car p35, Patsy Slevin p37, Oz at Prospect Brewery p38, King's Head and blackboard p48, The Ship Inn and Newton Bay p51, heather landscape within photomontage p52, blind tasting p56, park bench p58, caravan p61, caravan p63, cooking and eating haggis p64, flat tyre and on the ferry to Islay p66, at Bruichladdich p68, Bruichladdich cask p70, in sports car and police p71, Guinness sign p82, in pub p83, hair salon p84, pub images pp85–6, beer p95, Royal Ale Store p97, Carlsberg plant p101, Windsor Castle images pp104–5, Tyrrells production pp112–13, James May bottling p116, Gwatkin p118, on buggy at Three Choirs p119, Oz and James p120, megakeggery p122, snapshots on Homebrew Challenge p123, empty glasses at Naish's pp124–5, Somerset Cider Farm p127, apple tree p129, apples on ground p130, Naish's Cider Farm pp131 (below), Naish's Cider Farm pp132–3, Somerset Distillery sign, pig, sheep, Oz and James pp134–5, Morris dancing p137, Oz and Sam Lindo in caravan p138, James's botanicals p141, caravan life pp142–4, in front of stainless steel at Wiston p153, blind tasting at Breaky Bottom p157 (above left, middle left and below right), Oz and James on cliff at Dover pp164, 165, 168, 172–3, food and cider at Naish's p167, car p169, gin on bunsen burner p170, watching whiskymaking pp176–7, car p179, Oz in anorak p186, images for Fawcett's, Prospect Brewery, The Ship Inn, BrewDog,

New Alloa Brewery, Bull & Castle, Worthington's, Windsor Castle Inn, Tyrrells, Three Choirs Vineyard, Naish's Cider Farm, The Somerset Cider Brandy Company, Camel Valley Vineyard and Breaky Bottom Vineyard pp188–9

SADLER'S BREWERY: Artwork p103

THE SOMERSET CIDER BRANDY COMPANY: Stills p134, apples on ground in orchard p135

THAMESIDE MEDIA: hop flowers and pears on page 3 (sourced from iStock), route map artwork p6, pub photomontage pp12–13, glass of beer p15, barley p17 (sourced from iStock), malt samples p20, glasses p21, grains p22, hop flowers p24 (sourced from iStock), beer p25, Thornbridge Hall p26, Kipling bottle p28, glass of dried malt p30, Jaipur bottle p31, barrel and kegs p41 (sourced from iStock), photomontage p42, Leventhorpe bottles and wine pp45–6, chalkboard p50, pub and postcard photomontage pp52–3, cap and bottle p59, bottles and glass of beer pp61–2, whisky glass p67, Irish pub and icons photomontage pp74–5, glasses of stout p78–81, crushed Guinness can p83, whiskey bottles p84, dartboard photomontage pp88–9, bottle p91, breakfast beer and spoon p92, beery Burton photomontage p93, artworks p94, cappuccino and lager devils and angel ales p99, lager and froth p100, glass p103, award of merit artwork p104, photomontage pp106–7, vodka bottle and glass, potatoes and crisps pp110–11, bottle and potatoes p115, perry bottle p117, grapes icon p121 (sourced from iStock), Homebrew Challenge photomontage p123, notebook photomontage p128, apples p129, Cornish pasty p136, Hogarth's Gin Lane and Beer Street (sourced from Wikimedia Commons, copyright free) p139, gin and tonic p140, caravan plans (based on a sketch by Oz and James) pp142–3, blind tasting bottles and rosettes p156, British Bulldog bottle and glass p158, Battle of Britain commemoration stamp p159, dried hops in glass p161, beers p165, crushed can p166, whisky glass p167, vodka bottle p169, sparkling wine p171, toucan drawing and stout glass p173, mug of tea p174, blackboard p175, timeline artwork p178–9, all beers pp180–1, Leventhorpe wines in garden p182, notebook p182, wine map artwork p183, grapes icon p183 (sourced from iStock), whisky glass, Redbreast, Green Label and Glengoyne p184, whisky map artwork p185, barrel icon p185 (sourced from iStock), glass of cider p186, cider map artwork p187, apple icon p187 (sourced from iStock), pear icon p187 (sourced from Shutterstock)

THREE CHOIRS VINEYARD: Wine bottles p119, vineyard p121, vineyard p170, vineyard p182

SIMON TOSELAND: Caravan in flood p91

TYRRELLS: Tractor in potato field p111, logo p114

WESTERHAM BREWERY: Robert Wicks p158 (credit James Boardman), Ian Strang and oast house in the wind p160 (credit John Millar), Ian Strang p189 (credit John Millar)